THE EXTREMISTS

THE EXTREMISTS

by Mark Sherwin

ST MARTIN'S PRESS, NEW YORK

TO MARY

Acknowledgments

The editors of St Martin's Press, on behalf of the late Mark Sherwin, wish to thank the individuals and publications listed below for permission to reprint material used in this book.

John F. Cronin, "Communism: Threat To Freedom," reprinted by permission of the Paulist Press, 401 West 59th Street, New York 19, N.Y. Victor Riesel, column in *The New York Mirror*. *National Review*, Publisher's statement in Vol. I, No. 1 (November 19, 1955). James Wechsler, REFLECTIONS OF AN ANGRY MIDDLE-AGED EDITOR, reprinted by permission of Random House, Inc., 457 Madison Avenue, New York 22, N.Y. Peter Viereck, book review in *The New York Times*. Walter Winchell, column in *The New York Mirror*. William Buckley, UP FROM LIBERALISM, Copyright 1959, reprinted by permission of Ivan Obolensky, Inc. AMERICA, the National Catholic Weekly Review, 920 Broadway, New York 10, N.Y., editorial. Karl E. Meyer, reprinted from an article in *The Progressive*, Madison, Wisconsin. Robert Welch, for permission to quote from the Bulletins of the John Birch Society. Gene Grove, INSIDE THE JOHN BIRCH SOCIETY, reprinted by permission of Fawcett Publications, Inc., 67 West 44th Street, New York 36, N.Y. Eric Hoffer, THE TRUE BELIEVER, reprinted by permission of Harper & Row, Publishers, 49 East 33rd Street, New York 16, N.Y. Dr. Russell Kirk, for permission to quote from an article which appeared in AMERICA, The National Catholic Weekly Review, February 17, 1962. Alan Westin, reprinted from an article in *Commentary*, 165 East 56th Street, New York 22, N.Y. Thomas Storke, *Santa Barbara News-Press*. *The Los Angeles Times*. *The San Diego Union*. Dr. Fred C. Schwarz, THE DISEASE OF COMMUNISM. Jack Gould, television review in *The New York Times*. L. H. Howell, editorial in the *Mississippi Panolian*.

The editors also wish to express their thanks to Charles Lam Markmann, Mr. Sherwin's collaborator on ONE WEEK IN MARCH and JOHN F. KENNEDY: A SENSE OF PURPOSE, for his assistance in preparing the manuscript of this book for publication.

Contents

THE EXTREMISTS

A speaker screams at an audience that the United States should immediately repeal the income-tax law, but should spend unlimited billions on making more hydrogen bombs so that we can destroy Russia at once.

Another tells a credulous group that the fluoridation of drinking water is an anti-Christian evil and part of the great Communist conspiracy to brainwash America.

A handsome young man with flashing, fanatical eyes assures his listeners that all our problems can be solved by returning to the principles of Adolf Hitler.

But another fierce young man promises to assassinate all Nazis as fast as they reveal themselves.

A retired candy manufacturer says Dwight D. Eisenhower is a dedicated and conscious agent of the Communists.

A gentle and persuasive young man, who admits he once dabbled in left-wing activities but says he is now a realistic American patriot, asks his listeners to consider seriously whether it is better to be Red than dead.

A housewife uses the Scriptures to "prove" that segregation was ordained by God.

A Negro group abandons Christianity and demands that the United States set aside several states to set up a pure Negro community where the black man will have nothing to do with the white man.

This is the anatomy of Extremism in the United States today.

1. What they are fighting

The Communist Party in the United States is a direct extension of the Soviet Government. It differs from all other extremist groups in that its source and inspiration, financial and ideological, are part of Russia's drive to communize the world. It is under constant vigilance by the policing agencies of the United States, as it should be, but it is also the straw man set up by Rightist groups to justify their own existence.

The Kremlin has made use of internal subversion, economic warfare, psychological warfare, diplomatic pressures and military action to pursue its objective. Since the end of World War II, the Communists have won, through direct or indirect military action, control of Latvia, Lithuania, Estonia, Poland, East Germany, Hungary, Bulgaria, Rumania, Czechoslovakia, Yugoslavia, Albania, China, North Korea, North Vietnam and Laos. Cuba was conquered by an internal revolution. Subversion is being used in the Latin-American countries. Diplomatic pressures and psychological indoctrination are being used in Europe and the Near East.

The African countries are being subjected to psychology, diplomatic pressures and economic blandishments.

The Communist Party began its acts of subversion and infiltration in the United States in 1919. Until 1935, it was relatively ineffectual, although noisy. It profited more from the publicity gained during the fierce anti-Communist drives of Attorney General Palmer in the early 1920s than from its own works.

The Great Depression, the unsatisfied needs of one third of a nation, the despair and the economic insecurity were a fertile soil for the propaganda of the Communists. Moscow ordered its cells in America to soft-pedal the talk of violent revolution and to go along with any social advances under the banner of "fellow-travelers." The Communists told their reluctant prospects that "we may have different methods, but we will travel together toward the same objectives —food, clothing, shelter and security of all working people." It sounded fine, and the Comintern, representing international Communism, quietly ordered its members to infiltrate every phase of American society. All this was done to gain a foothold in the United States, and to unite all countries against the growing common enemy—Fascism.

Father John F. Cronin, in his book, *Communism: Threat to Freedom*, recalls:

> Communist ideas were examined, and often welcomed, in academic circles. In reaction to the depression, the New Deal brought to Washington many persons of a liberal, experimental point of view. Since this group was strongly opposed to Nazism and Fascism, quite a few of them welcomed assistance from any quarter, including the newly "respectable" Communists.

At the same time, the Congress of Industrial Organizations was seeking help in organizing mass-production workers. Its leaders did not reject assistance from trained Communist organizers. The peace aspect of the Communist line appealed to many churchmen and pacifists. When the Soviet Union and the United States were allied against the Axis during World War II, certain government circles used every opportunity to glorify Russia and even communism itself.

While the Communist Party, U.S.A., in 1935 was small, it was well trained and steeped in the conspiratorial tactics of Lenin and Stalin. Its main activities were directed along three lines: increase in its own membership; infiltration of sources of power and prestige; and enhanced public influence through the front-organization technique.

For membership, it appealed to the idealistic, the embittered, and the disillusioned. To the idealist, it stressed the Marxist promise of a world of peace and plenty, obtained by a centrally planned economy. Those embittered by unemployment, racial or religious discrimination, or harsh treatment from employers were promised a chance to crusade for justice. The disillusioned could look forward to radical changes that would give them a new chance for success in life.

The organization of Communist-front groups was one of the most successful moves made by the infiltrators. A front group was one whose public purpose was respectable, often noble, in the areas of social reform, world peace or civil rights. Its membership and board of directors were generally non-Communist and beyond suspicion. But the working officers who really controlled the group were concealed Communists who guided the activities of the front toward Communist goals. In later years, the innocent dupes of

these fronts were to supply the main victims for the investigations of Joe McCarthy.

The Communist Party in the United States grew in
strength and influence, its membership at one time reaching 80,000. This did not take into account the fellow-travelers, the dupes and the true Marxists who were not members
of the party. Through its publications, such as the *Daily
Worker*, members of labor papers and "highbrow" magazines, the Party spread its doctrine into all areas of society
with the emphasis on anti-Fascism and anti-Hitlerism. It
had a simple formula for catching converts.

If you were against war; against Hitler; against Musso-
lini; against Franco; in favor of shorter working hours, social security, greater medical care, better housing and racial
and religious equality, then, said the Communists—"You're
with us."

However, on one black day in 1939, the Communist
Party in the United States suffered its severest blow—it was
the day that Stalin signed a non-aggression pact with Hitler. For the first time the dupes, the innocents and the
starry-eyed optimists saw the pragmatic, cynical policies behind the "profession of the best for mankind." Not only
were there resignations *en masse* from the party, but those
on the fringe, the fellow-travelers, the left-wing liberals
drew away in horror from the party that had betrayed
them.

When the war started and the Soviet Union was "on our
side," there was sympathy and admiration for the Russians'
stubborn and heroic resistance to Hitler's onslaught. But
the idealism was gone out of many, and, when the war was

over and Winston Churchill made his famous "Iron Curtain" speech at Fulton, Missouri, it was evident that Josef Stalin had not changed. There were still some who joined, but the Communist Party here began to slip in influence and numbers.

By 1962, according to Father Cronin, membership was down to 10,000 "and [the Party's] limited funds are dwindling in the face of prosecution under the Internal Security Act of 1950. Communists no longer hold places of power in government, labor or the academic world, or any other area they strongly influenced in the 1930s and 1940s."

It is not safe to leap to the other extreme, however, and assume that the Communist Party either is dead or dying or has lost its power or potential to inflict serious mischief in the United States. Gus Hall, head of the American Communist Party, is publicly optimistic about its possibilities. He told a West Coast rally that there are about 100,000 "state-of-mind" members who are ready to come out into the open when the time is at hand. His boss, Nikita Khrushchev, has called the Communists in the United States "a valuable arm of the international Red movement." It is estimated that there are some 300,000 professional Communist espionage agents in the world, and the United States has its proper share of them.

Because of the tremendous official pressures that have been placed on the Communist Party here, it has changed its method of recruitment. Rather than a party in which everyone is welcome, it has created of its shrunken membership a highly secret, highly disciplined cadre. Today it is more difficult to become a member of the party than it is to

join the Federal Bureau of Investigation. After a recruit has
filled out a detailed questionnaire, which includes a genealogy, he must be vouched for by old-time members. Then
the party conducts intensive investigations to verify all the
information. As one party member confided: "We are really
no longer a party. We are a combination of underground
cells that will some day form the nucleus of a party."

J. Edgar Hoover, whose F.B.I. is the official watchdog,
estimates that there still are some 200 known or suspected
Communist-front and Communist-infiltrated organizations.
"Many of these fronts, under investigation," he says, "are
national in scope with chapters in various cities. They repre-
sent transmission belts through which the Communist
Party furthers its conspiratorial designs." Hoover notes
that, in the various groups that have been infiltrated, there
are "some celebrated, self-styled pacifists, and some men of
wealth and prominence who have sometimes been unwit-
ting, but sometimes knowing, political shills and stooges of
deceitful Communist manipulators."

Complaining that his 6,000 operatives are not enough to
take care of the job, Hoover reveals:

> The Soviet intelligence services have reorganized, multiplied
> their contacts with the American people, and have become
> aggressively bolder in spearheading their espionage against
> the United States. The intelligence organizations of the sat-
> ellite countries, carefully coordinated under Soviet leadership
> and control, have gained increasingly in experience and ability.
> The current widespread ramifications of the Soviet bloc
> espionage networks which today extend throughout the entire
> United States have indicated a realistic need for a further

tightening of our security on the home front. While the Communists speak of peace, their intelligence setup is the most extensive in world history.

Hoover describes the official Red line in the United States. First, it paints a picture of a degenerated American society while lauding Communism as a panacea offering "all things to all men." Its second point is that a lasting international peace is possible as long as no one stands up to Communist aggression. Third is peaceful co-existence on Communist terms. Hoover also criticized those Americans who assume a negative attitude toward their own country, and the Rightists who are conducting their own private battle.

"They are against Communism," he says, "without being for freedom. They are against ignorance without being for education. They are against sin without being for God."

Attorney General Robert Kennedy also took a slap at the irresponsible Right when he said that a sense of "frustration about how to combat Communism was a contributing factor to the formation of such groups. They pose a hindrance instead of a help to the official agencies that maintain a vigil on American Reds."

Kennedy also believes that the greatest internal danger the United States faces from Communism is "the espionage of Communist-bloc countries, instead of the party itself. The Communist Party here poses no danger as a political organization. It has been disregarded by the American people. However, it is always under close scrutiny by the F.B.I. in the area of espionage and sabotage."

Victor Riesel, the labor columnist, who has genuinely
fought Communism all his life, is not so sanguine about
the weakness of the party. Financially, he says, the party is
as strong as ever. The Internal Revenue Service has charged
that the party owes the Government $500,000 in regular in-
come and excess-profits taxes. The party contends that it is
one of 140,000 tax-exempt organizations. Riesel also counts
818 Communist-front groups that flourished in the 1950s
and into the 1960s, and 166 publications of various kinds
that have been issued since the party "went underground."

In spite of the repressions and the legal prosecutions, the
"Communist Party has never been louder, lustier and more
active," Riesel wrote.

Folk singers and "Freedom dancers," friends of Lumumba
and Gizenga, veterans of Soviet brigades in Spain, singers of
the "Bourgeois Blues," college meetings and coexistence cha-
rades—take your pick. The Communist Party, U.S.A., which
chants that it is in chains, is living a lusty, gay life across the
land.

Nowhere else could it happen. Nowhere else could a party
which has been branded by a government run rallies drawing
12,000 and obtain free of any capitalist charge hundreds of
thousands of dollars worth of radio and TV broadcast time.

We will survive all this despite the ridiculous—sometimes
called the radical—right and the extremist—sometimes called
radical—left. We will survive because there is a militant middle.

I have logged the travels of the Communist Party leaders—
the Gus Halls and Ben Davises and others who no longer
bear any titles, but who refer to themselves merely as spokesmen for the Communist Party. I have noted down their trav-

els from Bowdoin College, Maine, to universities in Washington, Oregon, and California. I have counted almost 1,000 meetings, all the way from New York to the West Coast via Chicago and Detroit.

Somewhere this non-existent Communist Party has raised almost a quarter of a million dollars for travel, hotels, printing, lawyers, briefs, and appeals documents.

From where did this money come? Obviously from abroad and from 'business men' who love their trade with the Soviet bloc and from agents who have had it stashed away for years. All is tightly controlled from some secret central one-man headquarters. It directs a very smoothly functioning propaganda operation.

Whoever the Soviet representative may be, he has matters well in hand, I gather from a long document recently issued secretly by the Party. Rising above the line of duty, I read the ten thousand words.

It revealed that, immediately after the Supreme Court ruled that the Party must register as a foreign agent, one inner Party group wanted to dissolve the Party. Their plan then was to concentrate on gaining power only through unions. This would have meant abandoning the Party, its machinery, its hootenanies, its co-existence propaganda.

What everybody appears to forget is that the Communist Party of the U.S.A. is still a legal unit. What the law says simply is that it must register. And because it and its officers are defiant, it has become Martyrs, Inc. And not since the thirties has it had it so good.

It has been known for years that the Communists have gone respectable. They can no longer be easily identified by their slovenly dress, advocacy of free love, pie-in-the-sky promises and street-corner rantings. Rather subtly they tell you that Mao Tse-tung is only an agrarian reformer; that it is better to be Red than dead, and that their only true enemy in the United States is the "crazy Right." It was Mrs. Elizabeth Gurley Flynn, a veteran Communist leader, who immediately came to the defense of Dwight Eisenhower and John Foster Dulles after they were accused by Robert Welch of being Communists.

How few new dupes the Communists will find with their new public image is shown by surveys made in colleges and among younger people elsewhere. Almost all questioned said they saw through the disguise and were not impressed. Communism in America is clearly identified with the Soviet Union's drive throughout the world. No one doubted that American Communism was financed by Moscow, that the movement here is contrary to all that Americans stand for; that it is a completely foreign ideology and that in the most practical areas it has less to offer than what we already have in this country.

Americans of all ages became more united against Communism by the successes of the Soviet Union in space. They were shocked that for the first time in our history we had a potential enemy who might be more powerful than the United States. The situation left little room for tolerance of Nikita Khrushchev's American representatives.

While the vast majority of Americans felt that it was enough to remain on guard against the propaganda, promises and blandishments of the local Communists, and that official surveillance and action should be the province of responsible Government agencies, there were some who were impatient and hysterical.

With exaggerated fears and a lamentable lack of confidence in the Government, these people have formed organizations to fight Communism on their own wild and irresponsible level, and have themselves been used as dupes to press for ideas that have nothing to do with the battle against Communism.

This is the tragedy of the extreme Right.

2. The intellectual Right

The most revealing commentary on the unifying force binding the thousand or so groups of the far Right is that their greatest intellectual protagonist, William F. Buckley Jr., can define their objectives only in negative terms: anti-Communism abroad and anti-statism at home. With the smooth sincerity of a patent-medicine huckster on television, Buckley acknowledges sadly that it is a failing of the right-wing conservatives of today that they cannot fully agree on what they are for—only what they are against.

In spite of this obvious handicap, Buckley, erudite editor of *The National Review* and a persuasive public speaker, manages to get the message across. His manner is urbane to the point of slickness and civilized to the point of being suspected of too much sportsmanship toward his opponent.

One incident demonstrates this. Shortly after *The National Review* came out in November, 1955, Buckley visited T. S. Eliot in London. The poet apologized for not knowing of *The National Review*, explaining that "the only American publication I know well is *The New Leader* [a left-

wing, but strongly anti-Communist publication]." Eliot
went on to tell the startled Buckley that *"The New Leader*
seems to me the most brilliantly edited magazine in the
world." When Buckley got back to New York he called Sol
Levitas, the editor of *The New Leader,* to tell him what
Eliot had said.

Consorting with the enemy is one of Buckley's favorite
methods of spreading his views. He takes the practical position that, when speaking before a right-wing group, he is
making no new converts, but when he appears with James
Wechsler, editor of *The New York Post,* or Murray Kemp-
ton, one of its columnists, or Professor Arthur M. Schlesinger Jr., special assistant to President Kennedy, or Socialist Norman Thomas, he is drawing many liberals, who, he
feels, should be exposed as often as possible to some intelligent right-wing propaganda.

He gets special joy in using Wechsler, with whom he has
appeared in many debates, as a means of hurling a dart or a
barrage against the opposition. Writing in his publication,
Buckley tried to demonstrate that "there never was an age
of conformity quite like this one or a camaraderie quite like
the Liberals'. Drop a little itching powder in Jimmy Wechsler's bath and, before he has scratched himself for the third
time, Arthur Schlesinger will have denounced you in a
dozen books and speeches, Archibald MacLeish will have
written ten heroic cantos about our age of terror, *Harper's*
will have published them, and everyone in sight will have
been nominated for a Freedom Award."

Buckley combines the right-wing negative approach with
a consistently defensive attitude. "Conservatives in this
country," he wrote, "at least those who have not made

their peace with the New Deal, and there is a serious question whether there are others, are non-licensed nonconformists; and this is dangerous business in a Liberal world, as every editor of this magazine can readily show by pointing to his schools. Radical conservatives in this country have an interesting time of it, for, when they are not being suppressed or mutilated by the Liberals, they are being ignored or humiliated by a great many of those of the well-fed Right, whose ignorance and amorality have never been exaggerated for the same reason that one cannot exaggerate infinity."

Of their many debates, Wechsler writes in his *Reflections of an Angry Middle-Aged Editor*: "We have achieved something of the relationship of vaudeville performers. We also have, perhaps unhappily, a clear glimpse of each other's views, and our most earnest epigrams no longer come as a surprise; we are, it might be said, each other's straight man."

Wechsler evaluated Buckley the debater as "glib, erudite, alternately the perfect gentleman and the slugger, deferential and contemptuous, and rarely dull."

In his debates, his writings and his television appearances, Buckley reiterates a position he stated in the first issue of the magazine and, as Wechsler observes with admirable generosity: "One turns . . . to Buckley and his adherents for an examination of conservatism because, alas, it is almost they alone who hold aloft the flag and proudly bear the label. Like nervous liberals in politics who prefer to be known as 'middle-of-the-roaders,' few of those in public life who share Buckley's world view desire to be known as conservatives. The least modern Republican prefers to be identified as a champion of thrift, frugality, nationalism, and, on some days of the week, is even likely to proclaim that he is the true liberal."

Having been assured by the opposition that he is the true conservative, Buckley stated the following convictions in his magazine:

> It is the job of centralized government (in peacetime) to protect its citizens' lives, liberty and property. All other activities of government tend to diminish freedom and hamper progress. The growth of government—the dominant social feature of this century—must be fought relentlessly. In this great social conflict of the era, we are, without reservations, on the libertarian side.
>
> The profound crisis of our era is, in essence, the conflict between the Social Engineers, who seek to adjust mankind to conform with scientific utopias, and the disciples of Truth, who defend the organic moral order. We believe that truth is neither arrived at nor illuminated by monitoring election results, binding though these are for other purposes, but by other means, including a study of human experience. On this point we are, without reservations, on the conservative side.
>
> The century's most blatant force of satanic utopianism is communism. We consider "coexistence" with communism neither desirable nor possible, nor honorable; we find ourselves irrevocably at war with communism and shall oppose any substitute for victory.
>
> The largest cultural menace in America is the conformity of the intellectual cliques which, in education as well as the arts, are out to impose upon the nation their modish fads and fallacies, and have nearly succeeded in doing so. In this cul-

tural issue, we are, without reservations, on the side of excellence (rather than "newness") and of honest intellectual combat (rather than conformity).

The most alarming single danger to the American political system lies in the fact that an identifiable team of Fabian operators is bent on controlling both our major political parties—under the sanction of such fatuous and unreasoned slogans as "national unity," "middle-of-the-road," "progressivism," and "bipartisanship." Clever intriguers are reshaping both parties in the image of Babbitt, gone Social-Democrat. When and where this political issue arises, we are, without reservations, on the side of the traditional two-party system that fights its feuds in public and honestly; and we shall advocate the restoration of the two-party system at all costs.

The competitive price system is indispensable to liberty and material progress. It is threatened not only by the growth of Big Brother government, but by the pressure of monopolies—including union monopolies. What is more, some labor unions have clearly identified themselves with doctrinaire socialist objectives. The characteristic problems of harassed business have gone unreported for years, with the result that the public has been taught to assume—almost instinctively—that conflicts between labor and management are generally traceable to greed and intransigence on the part of management. Sometimes they are; often they are not.

No superstition has more effectively bewitched America's Liberal elite than the fashionable concepts of world government, the United Nations, internationalism, international atomic pools, etc. Perhaps the most important and readily demonstrable lesson of history is that freedom goes hand in hand with a state of political decentralization, that remote government is irresponsible government. It would make greater sense to grant independence to each of our states than to surrender U.S. sovereignty to a world organization.

How long ago did Buckley formulate his philosophy of "responsible dissent from the Liberal orthodoxy?" He does not quite recall. Born in New York City on November 24, 1925, the son of William Frank Buckley, an oil pioneer and a specialist in oil exploration in foreign countries, young Buckley attended the St. Thomas More School in London in 1933; St. John's Beaumont, Old Windsor, England, from 1938 to 1939; the Milbrook School in New York from 1940 to 1943, and the University of Mexico in 1943, and obtained his B.A. at Yale in 1950. Buckley Senior, who fathered four sons and six daughters, was a rugged Texan who became a lawyer and then went into the oil business. By the end of his life his oil holdings ranged from South America to Canada, from Israel to the Philippines.

At Yale the younger Buckley was editor of *The Yale Daily News,* but it was not until a year after his graduation that he created a furor on and off the campus with his book, *God and Man at Yale,* subtitled *The Superstitions of Academic Freedom.* In this book, Buckley was aroused not so much by what Yale did but by what it refrained from doing. It refrained, he said, from positively indoctrinating its students with a particular set of values. August Heckscher, in reviewing the book, said Buckley was "evidently an ardent Christian and a passionate devotee of individualism. He judges the rest of the alumni to be like him. Therefore, he maintains, the university should set as its chief goal the inculcating of Christianity and individualism."

Buckley maintained that the university not only should root out any influences which contradict the prevailing themes; it should engage only professors who actively subscribe to the established religious and economic orthodoxy. Almost as bad as a teacher who leads a student down false paths, Buckley held, is one "who lectures so dispassionately as to make highly reckless, on the basis of his course, any guess about his personal convictions on current issues. For the ideal of detachment is to be substituted that of devotion to dogma."

The book established Buckley, in the words of Peter Viereck's review in *The New York Times,* as "a young Saint Paul bringing us the long-awaited Good Tidings of a New Conservatism and Old Morality." Viereck also asked: "Is there no 'selfish materialism' at all among the National Association of Manufacturers as well as among the 'New Deal collectivists' [Buckley] denounced?"

Invitations to lecture swamped Buckley after the book's publication, and he was considered heir apparent to the unoccupied post of official philosopher of the Right. Three years later an item appeared in the column of Walter Winchell showing that Buckley was about to assume his rightful post. The item said: "Wm. Buckley, who wrote the best-seller, *God and Man at Yale,* has a sure click coming up in March. The title: *McCarthy's Enemies,* in which the author (who writes with an atomic punch) debunks his foes until they are ready for the garbage can." The book got the usual partisan reception. Wechsler wrote that Buckley was McCarthy's "emissary to the elite; he translated McCarthy's disorganized clatter into the patter of intellectuality just as, it might be said, he adeptly finds high social justification for every antisocial practice of the business community."

As McCarthy, Buckley's book and the hysteria faded from public attention, the observers of the Buckley phenomenon were mildly startled to find that he was a contributor to another book, called *Ocean Racing,* in which he revealed himself as an enthusiastic sailor who had participated several times in the classic Newport-Bermuda Race. When the surface was scratched further, it was discovered that Buckley also liked to ski, and occasionally took time off from his occupation and preoccupation to enjoy these sports. But the respite was short-lived. In that same year, 1959, he published *Up from Liberalism,* in which he resumed his attack on Liberals, using a rapier and a bludgeon.

Buckley charged that our politics, our education, our economics, our society in general are now largely under the control of those who have betrayed the nation's first principles. He named names, the usual ones—Mrs. Roosevelt, Adlai Stevenson, Schlesinger, Agnes Meyer, Averell Harriman, Paul Hoffman, Edward R. Murrow and such periodicals as *The New Republic, The Washington Post, The St. Louis Post-Dispatch, The New York Post* and much of *The New York Times.*

He again demonstrated his polemical skill at keeping his opponents off balance. He stated a credo when he wrote:

> I will not cede more power to the state. I will not willingly cede more power to anyone, not to the state, not to General Motors, not to the CIO. I will hoard my power like a miser, resisting every effort to drain it away from me. I will then use

my power as I see fit. I mean to live my life an obedient man, but obedient to God, subservient to the wisdom of my ancestors; never to the authority of political truths arrived at yesterday at the voting booth. That is a program of sorts, is it not? It is certainly program enough to keep conservatives busy, and liberals at bay. And the nation free.

Buckley is a devout Roman Catholic, but in the matter of his Rightist feelings, his rugged individualism, he proved himself to be somewhat of a dissenter. Pope John issued an encyclical in July, 1961, urging that underdeveloped areas should be aided. It also said that the advantages of socialization and state welfare programs should be accepted provided that the atmosphere of freedom of the personal initiative of individual citizens was not reduced.

In his *National Review*, Buckley called the encyclical "a venture in triviality." His editorial said the encyclical "took insufficient notice of the most obtrusive social phenomena of the moment." It said the social phenomena were "the continuing and demonic successes of the Communists; the extraordinary well-being that such free economic systems as Japan's, West Germany's and our own are generating, and the dehumanization, under technology-cum-statism, of the individual's rôle in life."

The encyclical, which covered a broad area of social justice, was entitled *Mater et Magistra*. The *National Review* carried an item that said: "Going the rounds in Catholic conservative circles: 'Mater, si; Magistra, no.' "

America, the highly respected and influential Jesuit weekly, said that to imply that "Catholic conservative circles accepted the Church as Mother, but not as Teacher, was slanderous." It continued: "So-called Catholic conservatives may be confused about this or that principle of Catholic social teaching; but they are not disloyal. However embarrassing it may be for some of them to discover from *Mater et Magistra* that their brand of conservative thinking can in some respects scarcely be reconciled with Pope John's teaching, they will accept it with filial respect . . . It takes an appalling amount of self-assurance for a Catholic writer to brush off an encyclical." The editors then suggested that *The National Review* owes "its Catholic readers and journalistic allies an apology."

Buckley was furious over the Jesuit attack. He charged that *America* was "impudent" in its attitude; that it was arguing not with the merits of *The National Review*'s comments, but "with our presumption in writing at all—on the extraordinary grounds that I am a Catholic, and that to have written, under the circumstances, is disrespectful." He pointed out that *The National Review*'s editorial was the position of its editorial board, made up of Catholics, Protestants and Jews. The magazine, he said, was no more Catholic because its editor is Catholic than the Administration is Catholic because the President is Catholic.

On the National Broadcasting Company's *Open Mind* program Buckley took the position that this is no longer a Protestant country, therefore Catholics and Jews ought to be treated on a par with the Protestants. He expressed admiration for the manner in which the Jews conduct themselves as a minority and charged that the Catholic population "is supine beyond belief. I don't think that they can mobilize in behalf of themselves, certainly not consistent with their political resources and not even consistent with the demands of pride."

To illustrate his point he cited the case of Paul Blanchard, who had written a series of pieces for *The Nation* "which were, roughly speaking, the kind of things Gerald L. K. Smith runs against the Jews. A few months after this series, which got considerable notoriety, *The Nation* celebrated its 90th anniversary and invited, and got there at its banquet, three or four members of the Supreme Court, half the governors, practically every Liberal academician in town—it was a large party, needless to say. This kind of thing would have been unheard of if there had been an equivalent attack on Negroes or on Jews or indeed on Holy Rollers. So I think that the Catholics are supine politically."

Again Buckley showed that he could be persuasive and apparently sincere by beginning with a false premise and going on to exaggerate the results. Blanchard's articles attacked not Catholics but the hierarchy, and no one but a Buckley would equate *The Nation* with Gerald L. K. Smith in any frame of reference.

It is the nature of the man, even at his most amiable moments, to give the appearance of an insufferable intellectual snob. He came out a poor second in a joust with Jack Paar, who listened with pained bafflement to Buckley's ambiguous but lofty prose. After Buckley had concluded his lecture to Paar and the great television audience with a condescending, "I hope you learned something," Paar spoke a harsh truth to many of Buckley's own followers when he said: "I listen to him and I don't know what the hell he's talking about. It's my shortcoming . . ."

Actually it was not Paar's shortcoming alone. Most of those on the far Right who like their solutions simple have referred to Buckley as a scrambled egg-head. They suspect

him as a man of too many parenthetical phrases and qualifying clauses. There are others, however, who are proud of
the fact that the far Right at last has an egg-head who is
the master of the specious argument, skilled at the soaring
rhetoric that gives an impression of depth, and the apparent
intellectual sincerity that has captured the imagination of
an increasing number of college men and women.

How easy it is for Buckley to blur all the issues and
sweep away all the contradictions of his own platform and
those of the countless other right-wing groups when he replies to the question: "What is a conservative?"

"A conservative," he replies with mystic earnestness,
"feels that he knows the way to personal serenity. For him,
it comes through spiritual and intellectual and moral recognition of the facts of life."

Could anyone ask for more?

3. The urbane Right

Senator Barry Goldwater of Arizona is the knight in shining armor, the darling and the idol of the Right. He is also its prisoner. His followers and admirers extend in their political and emotional attitudes from the true conservatives just to the right of Eisenhower and Nixon, to the absurd intellectual Siberia of Robert Welch and his John Birch Society.

Not since Senator Robert Taft has a conservative been so adored, sought after and touted as the savior of his country and his party. To the charge by the Liberals that he wants to repeal all social legislation passed since 1933, Goldwater replies: "When history is written, we Conservatives will be called the Liberals, since we are truly concerned with the freedom and right of the people. The so-called Liberals profess to be humanitarians, yet they admit that 17,000,000 people go to bed hungry every night, and that 30 percent of our people are poorly housed and clothed. If, after 30 years of their Welfare State legislation, these facts are so, what is their answer? Is it for more giveaway legislation?"

There is nothing of the rabble-rouser about Goldwater, but he is articulate to the point of glibness, exudes honesty and sincerity and is regarded by many women as devastatingly handsome. On the speaker's platform his lean, swiftly moving six-foot frame, his white hair, his relaxed, agreeable manner and his impeccable attire give conviction to his words. His necktie is broidered with a small "G," on one finger is a gold ring of three bands showing that he is a 33d-degree Mason, and his cuffs are held together by small gold elephants with sapphire eyes. These were good-luck pieces given to him by his wife, Peggy.

He is distinguished from most Old Guard members in that he enjoys a joke about himself. He likes to repeat the anti-Goldwater remark made by Senator Hubert Humphrey: "Senator Goldwater is such a handsome dog that he's just been signed to make a movie by a big studio—18th Century-Fox." And in an exchange on the Senate floor with Democratic Leader Mansfield he said: "Like you, I'm a Westerner, accustomed to standing lonesome in the desert with just the wind and the Lord around. Here in the Senate the wind is around all right, but the Lord seems to be missing."

But after the gentle humor has been disposed of and he peers at an audience through horn-rimmed spectacles that enhance the desert tan of his face, Goldwater evokes wild cheers when he declares that "the country has been caught up in a wave of conservatism that could easily become the political phenomenon of our time." Consciously or unconsciously he borrows the title from Anne Lindbergh's fascist book when he says that "conservatism is the *Wave of the Future* and has come to life after 30 years of apathy. It is young, virile and alive."

Goldwater's power lies in his philosophy of taking a clear position and stating it clearly. He calls himself an "unabashed, unapologetic conservative." When the United States was trying to negotiate with Castro for the release of American prisoners after the Cuban invasion blunder, Goldwater described the action as a "disgusting, sickening spectacle of our America groveling before a cheap, dirty dictator." Audiences throughout the country heard him ask: "How sick do we have to get? How rotten can we be? How low can we sink as Americans before we rise up? Our heritage demands more than this. The memory of our men who have died fighting demands more than this."

He has toured the country damning the Kennedy Administration for what it did and what it did not do. "If the President would make up his own mind, he'd be better off," Goldwater declared. "Instead he's being influenced by these academic minds around him. All we are getting are groupings of beautiful English. Kennedy has done an about-face on everything. I can't think of anything Mr. Khrushchev wants more than irresponsible fiscal policies such as we are under today where we don't even know what the deficit will be next year."

He mistrusts the United Nations, saying: "I am opposed to submitting major policy decisions to a forum where the opinions of the Sultan of Yemen count equally with ours." Occasionally he is guilty of stating a vague position in grandiose terms, as in the case of the satellite countries of Europe: "I believe we should encourage the captive peoples to revolt against their Communist rulers. This policy must be with caution and prudence as well as courage."

As the spokesman for the Right, the heir of Robert Taft and the Liberty League, Harding and McKinley, Goldwater offers as an alternative to the "ever-expanding Welfare State": the policy of "the less government the better."

"My whole argument," he says, "is based on the historic concept that man can do best for himself, and, when he can't do it for himself, then and only then should government step in and do it for him."

Goldwater is against deficit spending and favors states' and cities' rights. He urges the Federal government to leave to states and cities such programs as public housing and urban renewal, laying himself open to charges by Liberals that this is another example of an unrealistic attitude. Where is the money to come from? they ask. Goldwater, who has been known to quote such conservative philosophers as Edmund Burke and Russell Kirk, swiftly denies that he is either an egg-head or a profound political thinker. "I am not a philosopher," he says. "I am a salesman trying to sell the conservative view of government."

Reporters who have followed him on the Republican circuit and at mass rallies staged by his most enthusiastic followers, the Young Americans for Freedom, have described him as a consummate actor and a political figure of star quality. He can "mumble and stutter" through a carefully prepared and rehearsed speech when the type of audience calls for it, or he can toss away a prepared speech and deliver it flawlessly "in an inpromptu manner." He possesses the instincts of the traditional vaudevillian who felt his audience and adjusted his act to fit the variations of time, intellect and geography. But, like the vaudevillian, Goldwater keeps the same tried and true act.

He has been called a Janus personality—his thinking goes back to McKinley—but in every other way he is the most modern man in politics today. His versatility is awesome to observe. He is a businessman, politician, jet pilot, folklorist, explorer and athlete. As a major general in the Air Force Reserve he is the very model of one, with almost 8,000 hours of flying time and an enthusiasm for flying that would match that of a new graduate of the academy.

He is an heir to wealth as well as to the rugged individualism and self-reliance that came to him from a pioneering family. Goldwater's grandfather staked his claim in Arizona Territory before it even had a capital. The grandfather, Michael Goldwasser, was born in Konin, Russia, sometime in the 1820s and went to England at the age of 27. He met a girl in London and married her. They were both Jewish, but decided to anglicize the family name. When news came of the discovery of gold in California, Michael, later called Big Mike, shipped out in 1852 for San Francisco with his brother, Joseph. They did not pan for gold. They sold hard liquor and equipment to the miners in Sonora. The brothers prospered, going southward to Los Angeles, where they ran a pool hall, bar and smoke shop in the Bella Union Hotel.

Big Mike liked the excitement of the gold frontier although he never had the desire to prospect for gold. Like many Jews from Eastern Europe he wanted to be a merchant—a big merchant. When he heard of a new gold strike in Arizona, he hitched up his mule to a wagonload of goods and set off as a peddler serving miners' camps. When the business became too big to handle from a wagon, he set up a trading post at a riverside and called it Ehrenberg, after a family friend. Ten years later, in 1870, he opened a bigger store in Phoenix, sold it to set up another one in Prescott, and continued to prosper and expand. Mike had become so assimilated that at one time he had trading posts in the boom-bust towns of Tombstone, Seymour and Bisbee, where the town's first lynch mob stopped at his store to get a suitable length of rope. The family recalls that grandfather was a strong, resourceful man, a stern disciplinarian and a rugged individualist.

When age and illness slowed him down, Mike retired to California in 1885, leaving all the stores to his three sons, Morris, Henry and Baron.

Morris soon was fascinated by politics and went at it in typical Goldwater fashion. He became a conservative Jeffersonian Democrat and helped organize the Democratic Party in Arizona. He became mayor of Prescott and held that office for a record 26 years. He was vice president of the 1910 constitutional convention that brought Arizona into the Union and served in both houses of the state legislature. Goldwater admits that his uncle Morris had profound influence upon him, and recalls with pride that he is one of the great legends of the family and state.

Baron, Goldwater's father, was more the merchant than the politician. He left Prescott in 1895 to open another Goldwater store in Phoenix, where he met Josephine Williams, a nurse from Chicago who had come to the healing climate of Arizona for the sake of her lungs, wasting with tuberculosis. The family recalls that doctors had given the frail but courageous woman only a few months to live. But

Baron felt otherwise. He married her, Goldwater says, after both decided that "she didn't want to die." As this book is written, she is a hale and impressive woman of 85, a strong influence on her children and grandchildren, and, as one biographer put it, "the most gentle matriarch in Arizona."

Barry Morris Goldwater, the oldest of three children, was born in Phoenix on January 1, 1909. His sister, Mrs. Bernard Erskine, the youngest, recalls the "wide-open" Goldwater *ménage* where Barry and his younger brother, Robert, "were given free reign to their capacity for mischief—even when summer-night water fights ended up with lawn hoses spurting about indoors. He grew up in the style of a bourgeois Huck Finn; he never wore shoes regularly until high school, and amused himself by tossing pats of butter at the ceiling."

Although their father was Jewish, the children were raised as Episcopalians. There seemed to be no overt conflict in this situation. Young Barry, after reading his first issue of *Popular Mechanics*, became an eager hobbyist. By the time he was 12, he had assembled his own radio transmitter and had qualified for a license as a ham operator. His sister relates that he wired everything in sight, from toilet seats to his bedboard. He discovered a fascination with guns, became a crack shot and created an incident that is still recalled. One evening, to celebrate his mother's birthday, he took a home-made 10-gauge shotgun, mounted on wheels, to the second-floor porch of the family mansion, which faced the Central Methodist Church across the way. He loaded the piece with live ammunition and released the charge at the moment when vespers were over. The porch

railing was demolished but fortunately none of the wor-
shippers was hurt. Barry said it was an accident.

The young man did not excel in scholarship, as his father
had wished. After one year at Phoenix Union High School,
where he got poor grades but was elected class president
and won honors in Latin, he was sent to Staunton Military
Academy in Virginia, where he got his diploma, was captain of the football team and won a medal as the outstanding cadet.

After Barry spent one year at the University of Arizona,
most of it behind the wheel of a dashing convertible, his
father died in February, 1929, and he returned home to
work in the store. For the benefit of all his young followers,
and even those students who oppose him, Goldwater admits and admonishes that "leaving college was the worst
decision I ever made."

There was nothing of Horatio Alger about his start in
the store. Although working behind the yard-goods counter,
he had the title of vice president and made full use of it,
roaming about and absorbing atmosphere and knowledge.
When he moved into the executive offices, he demonstrated
a profitable flair for merchandising. Under his guidance and
enthusiasm, the store developed from an ordinary middle-
class establishment into the Phoenix equal of a Neiman-
Marcus. One of his more imaginative innovations was the
marking of goods with cattle brands, the heraldry of the
frontier. He bottled and sold a fine brand of cologne under
the obvious name of Gold Water and started a national fad
in men's shorts covered with a design of ants under the
equally obvious name of "antsy pants."

Goldwater, now an inactive $12,000-a-year chairman of the board, is remembered by his employees as the man who paid average salaries; instituted a pension and a profit-sharing plan and shipped live mice through pneumatic tubes to the secretarial pool. Between practical jokes he managed to demonstrate a cheerful paternalism that went well with the workers.

The store, however, was not sufficiently demanding upon the abundant energy of the man. He played semi-professional basketball, retiring only after he suffered an injury to his left knee that gave him an almost imperceptible but permanent limp. He learned to pilot a plane and flew to all sections of Arizona to study Indian folk lore. He has an excellent collection of kachina dolls, images of the Hopi gods. He learned to be an accomplished rain dancer and made friends with remote tribesmen, many of whom still name their sons after him.

If Goldwater is to be envied his verve and his achievements, his list of accomplishments must include his virtuosity as an amateur golfer. The story of the Phoenix pro-amateur match of 1940 is still repeated in hushed tones in club houses where business men gather to boast and alibi. Goldwater was teamed with Sammy Snead, who appeared on the first tee attired in the finest fashions of the game, a fixed requirement among professionals. Snead was startled and dismayed when Goldwater stepped up wearing a soiled shirt, faded khaki trousers and paratrooper boots. Snead was mumbling something about why his partner could not afford even golf shoes, when he was further irritated by Goldwater's first tee shot, which he dubbed for 12 yards. Whether the dub was a deliberate typical practical joke or whether it was accidental need never be known, because Goldwater went on to birdie one hole and score eagles on two more. He and Snead finished well ahead of the field—Snead emotionally exhausted and Goldwater fresh and smiling.

In 1934, after a three-year courtship, Goldwater married Margaret Johnson, the daughter of a Borg-Warner Corporation vice president. They have four children.

When World War II broke out, Goldwater succeeded in getting an active-duty assignment with the Army Air Force although he was clearly ineligible. He was over age, and had a bad leg and a severe astigmatism. Sent, at first, to a non-flying job at Luke Field in Phoenix, he pressed and pushed until he got his wings. He ferried P-47s across the North Atlantic, was in action in the Mediterranean and China-Burma-India theaters and emerged at the end of the war as a lieutenant colonel. Despite his several ailments, Goldwater is regarded as quite fit for his age. Even in this area there is a remarkable facet. Goldwater is the possessor of a rare blood type, A-negative, and he has donated more than 50 pints.

When he returned to civilian life, Goldwater drifted toward politics in the most casual way. He went back to the store, but continued to pursue new hobbies. He spent six weeks with a group of friends mastering the dangerous rapids of the Colorado River, and took many pictures, which he published in two volumes. He made a collection of slides and took them on a lecture trip to praise the beauty of his beloved Arizona. After a while it seemed that everybody in the state knew Barry Goldwater. In 1930 he had joined the Republican Party, a sort of political dead end in

Democratic Arizona—a one-party state because its early settlers had migrated from Texas and the Deep South. By 1945, however, newcomers from the Middle West had reduced the Democratic advantage from a 12-to-1 ratio to 4 to 1. In 1949, Goldwater ran for the City Council on a nonpartisan ticket, coming in well ahead of his slate. The following year he managed the successful gubernatorial campaign of Howard Pyle and the Republicans became recognized as a force in the state.

A local Republican victory was not regarded as a groundswell, but the party took a daring step and put up Goldwater for the United States Senate in 1952. His opponent was the established Senator Ernest McFarland, the majority leader under President Truman. McFarland made a forthright campaign, standing on his Roosevelt-Truman record. Goldwater openly declared himself a conservative, denounced "waste and wild experiment in government" and appealed to the pioneer's traditional distrust of bureaucracy. While Eisenhower carried the state by 43,000, Goldwater won over McFarland, 132,000 to 125,000. He called himself the "greatest coattail rider in the campaign."

In his early days in the Senate, it was hard to discern whether Goldwater was just being cautious or whether he had accepted the traditional party discipline. He was rewarded with coveted assignments to the Labor and Interior Committees, quite an achievement for a freshman senator. In 1955 he was given the job of directing the Republican Senate Campaign Committee, and dispensed party funds to conservatives and liberals with equal enthusiasm. It was during those campaign tours, however, that he became convinced that the Republicans were neglecting the grass-roots

Taft followers who did not approve of Eisenhower's efforts to "shape a modern Republicanism." When Eisenhower was returned to the White House in a sweeping victory, but failed to win the Senate or House, Goldwater began to map out his own path in the party. He then proceeded to do "the hardest thing I ever did."

On April 8, 1957, he stood in an almost empty Senate chamber to make the break. He denounced Eisenhower's "betrayal of conservative Republican principles. The President subverts the American economy because it is based on high taxes, the largest deficit in history and the consequent dissipation of the freedom and initiative and genius of our people."

Even though the break with Eisenhower was subsequently healed on a personal basis, it remained wide on a party basis. Having taken his stand, however, Goldwater continued to state clearly how he felt on other issues.

He urged that the Government reduce its spending by ten per cent each year and gradually withdraw from all welfare areas. He is against the Social Security program, but is willing to compromise if it is made voluntary instead of compulsory. He has voted consistently against bills aiding depressed economic areas. He is against medical care for the aged. He is against the farm-subsidy program. After having called Walter P. Reuther "the most dangerous man in America—more dangerous than the sputniks or anything that Russia might do," he declared that he favors stronger unions, but ones that are more free. He favors right-to-work laws, toughened restrictions on secondary boycotts, and limitations on organizational picketing. Although he says there is nothing immoral about business firms that lobby for laws they want, he is in favor of a prohibition against union spending for political purposes.

Goldwater is a practical Rightist. He voted against federal ownership of Hells Canyon Dam in 1956, but he supported the billion-dollar, federally sponsored Upper Colorado River Storage Project, which will be of prodigious benefit to his Arizona constituents. To a question about the blatant contradiction, he replied with a knowing smile.

Goldwater could be called a modern isolationist. He mistrusts anything and everything foreign, but is reluctantly aware that the United States is a world leader and must remain in international affairs. He suspects the United Nations and would limit its power. He has suggested that the United States withdraw recognition of the Soviet Union. He would not give financial help to uncommitted neutrals and favors drastic reductions in the foreign aid budget. He has always boosted the Air Force and has consistently supported military spending, stating that he favors greater military and technical assistance to America's tried and true friends abroad.

There are no illusions in Goldwater's plans for the Republican nomination for the Presidency. He has repudiated Welch and has admonished the John Birch Society. Sometimes he is embarrassed by the absurdities of the extreme Right and cringes when he is equated with the late Senator Joseph McCarthy. There is truly no political likeness between the two. McCarthy was a cautious demagogue who confined himself to anti-Communism and was never associated with the extreme Right. As a Wisconsin politician, McCarthy was the poor man's friend to the point where he once insisted that farm price supports be set at 110 per cent of parity.

It is accepted routine for Goldwater to say that he has no plans for trying for the White House, but the pressures are evident all about him. His mail runs to about 800 pieces a day. His book, *The Conscience of a Conservative*, is approaching the million mark in sales even though it is only a repetition of his old speeches. His thrice-weekly column is syndicated in more than 100 papers and brings him more than $1,000 a month, which he donates to Trinity Episcopal Cathedral in Phoenix. He gets hundreds of invitations to speak in all parts of the country.

But Goldwater says: "I have no plans [for the Presidency]; no staff, no program and no ambition for it. Besides, I've got a Jewish name, and even though we now have a Catholic in the White House, I don't know if the country is ready for me. But the Republicans may have to run a dark horse. Rockefeller would be hard to sell in the Middle West. I would be hard to sell to the Eastern Seaboard, and Nixon would be hard to sell to anybody."

Of deep concern to Goldwater is the chaotic organization of the extreme Right and the clumsy political judgment of its leaders. There are between a thousand and two thousand groups, each grinding its own little vindictive axe and each dedicated to offending almost everybody. There is the fear among realistic Goldwater supporters that some day all these chattering, irresponsible groups may be forced to desert Goldwater unless he repudiates them first.

In the meantime, Goldwater has managed to be all things to all members of the far Right. His speeches were largely responsible for the election of Senator Tower in Texas, the first Republican Senator the state ever had. As a champion of states' rights he has won to his side many White Supremacists in the South, but he has alienated the Negroes. Labor, to protect itself from annihilation, would have to stand solidly against him. Critics of newspapers and television have charged that Goldwater and the far Right have received far more publicity and attention than the movement warrants.

Occasionally the Knight in Shining Armor does not disdain to wallow in a little mud, or, to mix a metaphor, deliver the low blow in the best McCarthy manner. He will do this only when he is out of the national press limelight and is addressing a small sectional group. Speaking before a crowd in Columbia, South Carolina, Goldwater indicated that Chester Bowles had been right in his opposition to the Cuban invasion and said that he had been transferred from his State Department post because he had been "right once too often." Then, as an afterthought, he observed that "the only thing worse than being right in Washington is being Protestant."

The New York Post commented that "perhaps this is the Senator's conception of a lively joke; conceivably he assumed that such a comment would not be quoted beyond the boundaries of South Carolina. Whatever the circumstances, it must be solemnly reported that Barry Goldwater isn't funny when he makes his appeals to the lowest prejudices of Southern reaction."

Goldwater's personality is his chief asset. His supporters on the lunatic Right will forever be a burden and an embarrassment. The sportsmanlike attitude he evokes was summed up by Karl E. Meyer, the liberal Democratic newsman for *The Washington Post*, when he wrote: ". . . We who disagree with Senator Goldwater may soon be glad that he is around. No one could seriously maintain that Goldwater is a seditionist or a malevolent demagogue. On the contrary, he is a decent, upright and thoroughly attractive politician. The groups he speaks for deserve a spokesman, and a good one. They could do far worse than Barry Goldwater."

But another political observer, Herbert Block, who draws his devastating cartoons under the name of Herblock, drew one that showed a ragged mother and her two underfed children listening to Barry Goldwater say to them: "If you had any initiative you'd go out and inherit a department store."

4. The respectable irresponsible

Robert Henry Winborne Welch Jr. is the most repudiated man in the United States. As leader of the extreme right-wing John Birch Society, as heir to the mantle of Joseph McCarthy, and as the witch doctor who knows the cure for all governmental ills, he does not seem to be getting the loyalty and respect of the right-wing thinkers and politicians who are riding on his coattails. This is a continuation of the paradox of the entire Welch phenomenon.

Welch has been publicly disowned by such conservative leaders as Senator Goldwater, Senator Tower, Representative Judd, Fulton Lewis Jr., author Russell Kirk, William Buckley and his *National Review*, Republican National Chairman William Miller and his own brother, James O. Welch. In the matter of his charges against former President Eisenhower, Welch has even repudiated himself.

The Eisenhower case hurled Welch into the public spotlight when it was charged he had called Eisenhower a card-carrying Communist. Welch denied this. What he had actually written was that "Eisenhower is a dedicated, conscious agent of the Communist conspiracy."

In spite of the repudiations, Welch is still the actual as well as spiritual leader of the John Birch Society and still carries the word to all sections of the country. He travels alone, secretly, and even his chapter chiefs are not certain when he will arrive until shortly before he comes to town. On these occasions he stays in a private home that is seldom known until he meets his chapter leaders. There is a significant resemblance to the Communist cells in the chapter organization of the Birch Society. Each group has between ten and 20 members and a leader who is appointed, not elected; each member is given a single task in carrying out the society's program in the community. The members are responsible directly to the leader and only the leader speaks to Welch.

At public meetings Welch adheres to a fixed 90-minute address. He seems unaware of his audience, paying strict attention to his lecture cards, as if he were seeing them for the first time, although the speech is the same almost word for word. Yet he is thoroughly aware of his audience, which is made up only of loyal Birchers and their true friends. At one meeting there was a mild distraction when an attendant walked through the aisles searching for a doctor who was wanted in an emergency case. Welch looked up from his cards, glared at the audience, and asked why the man was walking around like that. Without waiting for an answer Welch told his audience: "This kind of disturbance is a typical dirty Communist trick."

His speech consists of the admonition that Americans should become "Americanists" dedicated to fighting Communism—beginning by taking a closer look at their neighbors. He encourages this sinister suggestion by saying that it worked successfully for the Communists and it should work well for anti-Communists. He tells his eager listeners that Communists can be found everywhere—in Harvard and in the pulpits—and that the enemy must be understood by what he calls the "principle of reversal"—which holds that everything the Communists seem to be they are not, and virtually everything they seem not to be they probably are. His audience listens to these words of wisdom with never a dissent—dissenters are not permitted in the hall. There are no question-and-answer periods. Of all the demagogues who have strayed across the American scene, Welch is the most colorless, the most furtive, the most defensive, and yet it is acknowledged that after he delivers one of his set speeches the divisions in the community he has just left are even more sharply and bitterly drawn.

A man of his type generally evokes some satire from the opposition. This has not been of the highest quality. The Houston Gridiron Club put on a skit entitled *Jane Smirch*; two disk jockeys started the John Burp Society with Robert Belch as the boss; and someone suggested that the Russians should start a John Borshcht Society. But the deadliest piece of humor, although unconscious, was supplied by an unknown secretary. She was approached by a Birch Society leader who wanted to hire the hall where she was employed for a meeting. He explained to the young woman that his group's slogan was "less government and more responsibility." She looked at him suspiciously and said: "What are you guys, anyway, Communists?"

This man who equates democracy with "mobocracy" and

whose posture on government and economics is to the right of King Louis XIV was born in 1899 on a North Carolina farm. Most of his paternal ancestors were men of the soil or Baptist preachers and were able to trace their genealogy to Miles Welch, who came to this country from Wales in 1720.

He describes his early youth as being spent "in the intellectually restricting bonds of the unusually narrow Southern Baptist Fundamentalism." He managed to wrench himself sufficiently free from these restrictions to spend four years at the University of North Carolina and then entered the United States Naval Academy in 1917. After one academic year he left, having achieved a standing near the top of his class. He explained his departure from Annapolis on two grounds: the war was over and he could not perform the service for his country for which he had joined the Navy, and he wanted to become a writer. Somehow the writing career was neglected and he entered Harvard Law School, where he again achieved fine grades, but withdrew after two years. He joined a candy manufacturing company, headed by his brother, with factories in Massachusetts and California. During World War II he served on the candy-industry advisory committee of the Office of Price Administration. He campaigned actively for Eisenhower in 1952. About that time one of his friends described him as a compulsive speaker. After years of groping for a subject to speak about compulsively, Welch found Communism. Perhaps this was the best subject for him because he found so many willing listeners, especially when he added zest to a commonplace theme by compulsive exaggeration. He found he was getting a better audience with the shotgun technique of spraying in all directions rather than with the single target aim of a rifle.

In December, 1954, he began circulating a letter to intimate friends in which he expressed severe opinions concerning the purposes of some of the top men in Washington. He said, among other things, that "the final straw that prompted my letter was the visible betrayal of the Republican Party by this so-called Republican Administration in the congressional elections which had just taken place. The deliberate use of Administration influence and the tricky maneuvers of Administration spokesmen, to bring about the defeat of stalwart Republican Congressmen and Senators, and to turn both houses of Congress over to the more left-wing Democrats, were entirely obvious."

Through revisions and additions the letter grew to 302 pages (80,000 words) and became known as *The Politician* or the *Black Book*. In it, Welch reviewed 40 Eisenhower appointments and saw a suspicious pattern. Excerpts from *The Politician*, placed in the Congressional Record, show that Welch wrote: "In my opinion the chances are very strong that Milton Eisenhower is actually Dwight Eisenhower's superior and boss within the Communist Party . . . I personally believe Dulles to be a Communist agent who has had one clearly defined role to play; namely, always to say the right things and always to do the wrong ones."

After declaring that it was his "firm belief that Dwight Eisenhower is a dedicated, conscious agent of the Communist conspiracy," Welch went on: "For the sake of honesty, however, I want to confess here my own conviction that Eisenhower's motivation is more ideological than opportunistic. I personally think that he has been sympathetic to ultimate Communist aims, realistically willing to use Communist means to help them achieve their goals, knowingly accepting and abiding by Communist orders and consciously serving the Communist conspiracy for all of his adult life."

Welch asked how a man born in the American Midwest, who went through the United States Military Academy, could ever become a convert to Communism, and gave the answer:

Those converts are most likely to occur among warped but brilliant minds, which have acquired either by inheritance or circumstances a mentality of fanaticism. And it should be no surprise to anybody that Eisenhower was raised with this mentality of fanaticism, for as recently as 1942 his mother was arrested for participating in a forbidden parade of Jehovah's Witnesses. But whereas in most historical cases fanaticism takes the form of outspoken promotion of the fanatic's cause, at whatever personal cost, the Communists have sold their converts the fundamental principle that the goals of their fanaticism can best be achieved by cunning deception. Everything Eisenhower has done for the past 18 years can be fitted into the explanation based on that type of mentality. And I do not believe that the events of his personal story during those 18 years can be satisfactorily explained in any other way.

The Communists can now use all the power and prestige of the Presidency of the United States to implement their plans, just as fully and openly as they dare. They have arrived at this point by three stages. In the first stage, Roosevelt thought he was using the Communists to promote his personal ambitions and grandiose schemes. Of course, instead, the Communists were using him; but without his knowledge or understanding of his place in their game. In the second stage, Truman was used by the Communists, with his knowledge and acquiescence, as the price he consciously paid for their making him President. In the third stage, in my own firm opinion, the Communists have one of their own actually in the Presidency. For this third man, Eisenhower, there is only one possible word to describe his purposes and his actions. The word is "treason."

Absurd and irresponsible charges flew in all directions, including the Congress, which, Welch said, had been brought into line, and the United States Supreme Court, which was "strongly and almost completely under Communist influence." He advocated the impeachment of Chief Justice Earl Warren, the repeal of the income-tax law, an end to the North Atlantic Treaty Organization and foreign aid, the abrogation of all cultural relations with the Soviet Union, restrictions of collective bargaining and an end to all civil-rights programs. He described the civil-rights movement as similar to Communist action in China. He called Dag Hammarskjöld "one of the most contemptible agents of the Kremlin ever to be supported by the American taxpayers." He charged that the outlawing of school segregation was part of the plan of that "nest of Socialists or worse, the Supreme Court, to subvert the nation and make it ripe for merging, without struggle, with Russia."

He coined a word, *Comsymps*, which, he said, is a "beautiful word, because you don't have to say how much the person is a Communist and how much he is a sympathizer." He used that word to attack the Protestant clergy in general, charging that at least three per cent of Protestant ministers are Comsymps as against one per cent of the Catholic priests.

"The largest single body of Communists in America is our Protestant clergy," he told a crowd in Shreveport, Louisiana, explaining that "Protestant ministers do not become Communists, but Communists become Protestant ministers."

When *The Pilot*, official organ of the Catholic Archdiocese in Boston, challenged him to name 50 priests who he believed were Communists or Communist sympathizers, Welch admitted that his figures on the Catholic clergy were "simply pulled out of a hat, a complete guess." Dr. Russell Kirk, ultra-conservative author and educator, wrote that "Ever since he [Welch] founded his Society, he has done more to injure the cause of responsible conservatism than to act effectively against Communism." Welch never further explained his remark on the Catholic clergy and brushed away Dr. Kirk's denunciation with another outburst against Comsymps.

When Welch is irked by strong words against him, he departs from his monotonous norm and acts like a tiger. After Richard Nixon had called him an "irresponsible demagogue with a dictatorial point of view," Welch went before an audience, boasted of his "fanaticism" and described himself as the "hard-boiled, dicatorial and dynamic boss" of the Birchers. He told the astonished gathering that he operated as a monolithic force and that the Birch members either accepted assignments without question or got out. All decisions, he said, are made at the top (he's the top) and are passed down through a chain of command. Then he quietly resumed the monotonous recital of his regular 90-minute lecture, cue cards and all.

Welch likes to pose as a modest man, when actually he is secretive. While lesser lights in the Birch Society will grant interviews or extend civilized courtesies to the press, Welch has rarely talked to reporters, convinced that there is a Communist (what other kind is there?) conspiracy against him within the press, radio and television.

He was sorely disappointed when such obvious non-Communist groups as the Elks' Club and the Athletic Club of Atlanta refused to let him hire their halls. He wound up in the North Atlanta Baptist Church, where he told a crowd of a thousand that President Kennedy was not so much a captive of the Communists as the previous administration had been "but I still don't like the continuing appeasement." By this time Eisenhower had decided to fight back. The former President was cornered by a group of reporters as he completed a golf game in Palm Springs, California, and replied rather mildly: "If I thought the American people thought that I was anything but a dedicated enemy of Communism, I would certainly be disappointed."

After his Atlanta experience, Welch was more careful in selecting his rostrums. He did not wish to be turned down publicly. But he was deeply hurt when two prominent Texas clergymen assailed him. Dr. William Elliott, pastor of the largest Presbyterian Church in the South, warned his congregation in Highland Park, near Dallas, that the tactics of Welch and his Birch Society could "create a climate of fear in which Americans would be afraid to voice their opinions." The Rev. William H. Dickinson

Jr., pastor of the largest Methodist Church in the nation, also in Highland Park, denounced Welch and his crowd for "reckless name-calling."

Welch recoils when he is attacked and sometimes he forgoes public appearances for a short time to bind his wounds and sulk.

He does his work secretly from a two-story brick office building in Belmont, Massachusetts. He gave in to "the pressure of chapter leaders and prospective members" and dashed off an autobiography, which avoided any stuffiness and, after reciting the statistics of birth and education, concluded: "Has one wife, two sons, a Golden Retriever dog, and fourteen golf clubs—none of which he understands, but all of which he loves."

His brother, president of the candy company, felt that Welch was too busy with the Birchers to give enough attention to the business and asked him to choose between making candy or fighting Communism. Welch chose the Birchers and concluded a 20-year career that included posts as a bank director and seven years as a member of the board of the National Association of Manufacturers.

Undismayed by the failure of a prediction to come true —that the Russians were about to invade the United States —Welch decided in December, 1958, to formalize his action with an organization. He called 11 "public spirited and patriotic men" to a meeting in Indianapolis and gave them a two-day lecture on the international Communist conspiracy. He read profusely from the *Black Book*.

It is significant that, until that dreary day in December, the far Right had been represented loosely by men such as Goldwater, McCarthy, and Nixon, who were regular members of the Republican Party, and did not subscribe to any of the small extremist groups that were scattered loosely and parochially throughout the United States, creating little attention in the national press.

Welch and his 11 considered Goldwater or Nixon as possible leaders for this new group that was to be called the John Birch Society. He rejected both men (there is no indication that any of the 11 did any talking) because he doubted whether either could supply the "dynamic overall leadership needed to save this country." Then he told a little about himself. He spent his early days selling, and his first book, in 1941, was *The Road to Salesmanship*. His next dealt with the great ideological struggle and was called *May God Forgive Us*. He told his listeners that he had built a wide personal following through his business associations, the NAM and lectures.

He then proposed himself as the leader of the Birchers, not because he had compelling leadership qualities, he explained, but because "I just don't know where you, or all of us, are going to find anybody else to take the job." He pointed out that the extreme anti-Communists had had no rallying point since the death of McCarthy.

Although the 11 men have never been officially identified, Gene Grove, in his *Inside the John Birch Society*, says that it is probable that among them were: Dr. Revilo P. Oliver, a professor of classical languages and literature at the University of Illinois; W. B. McMillan, president of the Hussman Refrigerator Co., of St. Louis; Fred C. Koch, president of the Rock Island Oil and Refining Co., of Wichita; T. Coleman Andrews, one-time United States Commissioner of Internal Revenue; Colonel Laurence E.

Bunker, former personal aide to General Douglas Mac-
Arthur; Robert W. Stoddard, president of the Wyman-
Gordon Co., of Worcester, Massachusetts; Louis Ruthen-
burg, former president of Servel, Inc., of Evansville, Indiana;
A. G. Heinsohn, Jr., president of Cherokee Mills, of Sevier-
ville, Tennessee; and William J. Grede, president of Grede
Foundries, Inc., and a past president of the National Asso-
ciation of Manufacturers.

Four other men were mentioned: Adolphe Menjou, the
actor; John Beatty, Chicago industrialist; Ernest Swigert,
president of the Hyster Company and a past president of
the NAM of Portland, Oregon, and E. P. Hamilton, a
leader of the Wisconsin Manufacturers' Association. Apparently these men dropped out without an explanation
from Welch.

Welch pointed out that he was not publicly identified as
a racist, an anti-Semite or an anti-Catholic. He showed that
he was a stable, highly successful business executive who
had a mission.

It was then agreed to create the John Birch Society with
Welch as the undisputed leader. The objective was the sal-
vation of the United States from the dangers of the Communist conspiracy.

5. The John Birch Society

If John Birch were alive today it is not improbable that he would be a member, if not a leader, of the society that bears his name. An examination of his life indicates that Welch used the standards of uncompromising fanaticism and humorless dedication to select John Birch as the ideal of the Birchers.

Birch was a true believer. Eric Hoffer, America's newest philosopher, gives the following definition of a true believer:

"He's the man who, multiplied by thousands, is shaping the world to his image.

"He's a guilt-ridden hitchhiker who thumbs a ride on every cause from Christianity to Communism.

"He's a fanatic, needing a Stalin (or a Christ) to worship and die for.

"He's the mortal enemy of things-as-they-are, and he insists on sacrificing himself for a dream impossible to attain.

"He is today everywhere on the march."

Birch was born in Landour, India, in 1918, the son of a

missionary couple of the Baptist persuasion. When he was two years old, his parents returned to the United States, residing in New Jersey and Georgia. When he was graduated from the Baptist-controlled Mercer University in Georgia in 1939 as the top man in his class, the faculty sighed with relief because his fanaticism was already showing.

One classmate described Birch as "always a zealot, always an angry young man. He felt that he was called to defend the faith, but he alone knew what it was. He was always suspicious of dissent from his own philosophy." A professor of psychology at the school said: "He was like a one-way valve—everything coming out and no room to take anything in. He was always telling other people what was right. He was an impatient listener except in the classroom, where he listened with fierce attention."

This fierce attention was not merely a matter of learning, as it turned out. It was also a matter of policing the faculty for heresy. In his senior year, Birch organized a secret "Fellowship Group" in order to suppress a casual liberal trend at Mercer. With 12 fellow students he collected examples of "heresies" uttered by members of the faculty. In one instance, a reference to evolution, Birch whipped up a fury among some of Georgia's Baptist ministers that resulted in the trial of five men. The cases were eventually dismissed, but the school was forced to admonish Dr. John D. Freeman, who at the age of 75 had become a world-renowned Baptist leader. Dr. Freeman was accused of using a theologically "unsound" textbook. Shortly after, Dr. Freeman quietly retired from the school. One professor declared that the incident had destroyed him.

A year later Birch went as a missionary to China and was there when Japan attacked Pearl Harbor. He was trying to get to the American lines to enlist when one night a coolie came to him and told him that an American had fallen out of the sky. The American was Lieutenant Colonel Jimmy Doolittle, who was with a number of the survivors of the spectacular raid on Tokyo.

Birch led Doolittle and his group to safety. The unit later became the Fourteenth Air Force under the command of General Claire Chennault, who assigned Birch to air combat intelligence. The young missionary performed great feats of daring and earned the unreserved praise of Chennault, who said: "Birch was the pioneer of our field-intelligence net." He recalled that Birch had traveled as much as 100 miles behind enemy lines to radio back word on prime Japanese targets. He directed the construction of three airstrips within the enemy lines. As a reward he got the Legion of Merit, and posthumously got an Oak Leaf Cluster for "exceptionally meritorious service."

Some time later, Birch was transferred to the Office of Strategic Services and was assigned to a base at Sian in North China that was distinguished for its large number of scorpions. Comments and excerpts from the diaries of the men who served with him showed that Birch was a "loner with a somewhat overbearing manner and, considering the type of warfare, a needlessly strict disciplinarian." Major Gustav Krause, commander of the base, noted apprehensively that "Birch is a good officer, but I'm afraid is too brash and may run into trouble."

After the Japanese surrendered, Birch, a captain, led a routine patrol to discover how far south the Chinese Communists had penetrated. His outfit ran into a Chinese Communist force, and at this point there are varied versions of what took place.

One version has it that the Communist officer wanted to disarm Birch, who argued violently against it. Birch was seized and shot after his hands had been tied. The Communists then bayoneted him at least 15 times and threw his body on a heap of junk and garbage.

A Montana television executive who was in the same unit said the patrol ran into a force of Chinese Communists who were upset by "what seemed to them an unwarranted intrusion. Captain Birch, speaking in Chinese, chose to bluff his way out of a difficult situation. Harsh words led to insults and insults to arrogance."

Everyone admitted there was a great deal of confusion. It was only ten days after V-J Day and Major Krause recalled that his "instructions were to act with diplomacy." In those days it was not easy to tell friend from foe. There were tensions and skittish trigger fingers. Krause concluded that "Birch made the Communist lieutenant lose face before his own men. Militarily, John Birch brought about his own death."

John S. Sample, who served in the same outfit, said the remainder of the team was released and returned to Kunming after an arduous trip on foot that took several weeks. The sergeant in command received a citation as a result of the successful withdrawal.

Welch's obdurate attitude in selecting Birch as the official saint of the society cost him the support of General Albert C. Wedemeyer, a member of the American Security Council, a rigidly doctrinaire right-wing organization, whose stated purpose is to "prepare detailed studies and recommendations on key national security issues of vital interest to all Americans."

For a time Wedemeyer served as an adviser on Welch's *American Opinion,* but resigned because he did not feel that Birch was the kind of man who deserved the adulation Welch and the society were giving him. Wedemeyer, who commanded the China-Burma-India theatre of operations and was Chiang Kai-shek's chief of staff, "knew John Birch, as a captain, in China." He recalled that Birch "was one of a number of men who participated in operations in China, parachuting behind enemy lines."

Wedemeyer said: "Birch provoked the attack on himself. He was arrogant. I warned Welch not to make a hero of Birch. That's why I quit as an adviser. I think Welch is a dedicated fine American, but he lacks good judgment."

But Welch would not be moved from his unilateral decision. He called Birch the "first American casualty in that third world war between Communists and the shrinking free world." In one of his early appearances in Atlanta, he noted righteously that in the audience were Birch's parents, Mr. and Mrs. George Birch of Macon, Georgia, "proud members of the local chapter named after their son." Welch felt that he was vindicated in his choice, and Mr. and Mrs. Birch fervently agreed with him.

Having satisfied himself that Birch and his antecedents were perfect for his purpose, Welch proceeded with the organization of the society.

In the matter of discipline, Welch took the position that those joining the society would "do so because they believe in me and what I am doing and are willing to accept my leadership. Those members who cease to feel the necessary degree of loyalty can either resign or will be put out."

Welch felt so right and righteous about his position— that no one could and therefore no one should disagree with him—that he illustrated it with an irrefutable anecdote. He told the story of the minister who had preached a superb sermon that had moved his entire flock to a fervid determination to lead nobler and holier lives. Then the minister said: "And that's the Lord's side. And now to be fair, for the next half hour I'll present the devil's side. You can then take your choice."

Under Welch's monolithic setup, the society functions almost entirely through small local chapters with some 10 to 20 members, headed by a chapter leader who is appointed by headquarters in Belmont. Dues are whatever the chapter or members decide, but the minimum is $24 a year for men and $12 a year for women. Local chapters are expected to hold meetings at least once a month or more often if the chapter leader decides. Leaders, who can confer life memberships for $1,000, are expected to be in constant touch with their members between meetings in order to keep the group functioning at all times.

With a goal of a million or more members, and with contributions of large and small sums constantly pouring in, Welch made it his fixed policy that there would be no financial accounting "for reasons all will understand." He said any moneys the Birchers might raise would be an "awfully small drop in the bucket against what either the Communist propagandists or the Reutherite labor bosses are spending against us."

There are paid staff men with the title of coordinator

who are in charge of forming new chapters. Major coordi-
nators are the next *echelon,* supervising the work of organization and "keeping strict and careful control on what
every chapter is doing, and even every member of every
chapter so far as effective work is concerned." He is quick
to point out that his system may put one "in mind of the
Communist principle of the dedicated few as enunciated
by Lenin. And we are, in fact, willing to draw on all successful human experience in organizational matters, so long
as it does not involve any sacrifice of morality in the means
used to achieve the end."

Welch makes no secret of his admiration for Communist
methods and feels free to borrow or plagiarize because he
is on the right side of the battle. "The use of fronts should
not be left to the Communists alone. They worked well for
them and they can work well for the Birchers." He urged
his followers to create such fronts—"little fronts, big
fronts, temporary fronts, permanent fronts, all kinds of
fronts." As examples he gave: a Committee to Investigate
Communist Influences at Vassar College; a Petition to Impeach Earl Warren; Women Against Labor Union Hood-
lumism (to show the suffering of wives and mothers in
labor strife). "The aim of this plan is to make as much
noise and turmoil for our side so we can wake up a lot of
people."

To further the dissemination of the Birch idea, Welch
set out to establish reading rooms similar to Christian Science reading rooms, small and inexpensive, in as many cities, towns and villages and as rapidly as possible. These also
serve as rental libraries and include the Welch-approved
anti-Communist books and all the accepted anti-Commu-

nist periodicals. Originally *The National Review* and the Fulton Lewis Jr. radio program were suggested to Birchers, but since Lewis and Buckley have repudiated Welch and the society, these outlets are no longer on the approved list. However, *American Opinion, Human Events* and the *Dan Smoot Report* are still strong in the libraries.

The writing of letters was organized along lines learned from the Communists when Welch showed that the "Communists boast they can now land 50,000 individually written letters in Washington on either side of any subject within 72 hours." He said the Birchers, "with the million truly dedicated and controlled supporters, could make this look like peanuts."

An example of how this mass pressure was to be applied was given during a talk on the battle against fluoridation. Welch urged that there be a "continuous overwhelming flood of letters, not just to legislators or the Executive Department in Washington, but to newspaper editors, television and radio sponsors, educators, lecturers, politicians, foundation heads and everybody else whose opinions, actions and decisions count for anything. Such an outpouring of mail would give more courage to a lot of people who would prefer to be more clearly on our side, and would at least slow down the brazen advance of some of those on the other side. Never stop or slow down. Keep that up for months if necessary."

A part of the same operation, Welch said, is the gathering of petitions. "Goodness knows the Communists have proved their subtle value and effectiveness. We ought to outdo the Communists at least two to one at that game until we finally make petitions so overabundant and commonplace that they cease, for a while at least, to be a useful technique for either them or ourselves."

The enemy is not always recognizable to the ordinary patriot, Welch pointed out. "One of the hardest things for the decent American to realize," Welch said, "is that a secret Communist looks and acts just like anybody else, only more so. One that I know is one of the nicest men you ever met. Most of them are."

Welch urged his members to be activists at all times. "Get to work and learn to talk Russian," he commanded. Members should infiltrate all community organizations, such as parent-teacher groups, school boards, trade groups, discussion groups and chambers of commerce. "Take them away from the Communists," he says. Members should be trained and then become brazenly active in harrassment of pro-Communist speakers at church meetings, political gatherings and public forums. They should create local paper organizations such as a Committee Against Summit Entanglements; College Graduates Against Educating Traitors at Government Expense and Committee Against Fluoridation.

Between front organizations and intensive letter-writing the Birchers have covered every controversial subject that has come up since their inception. Because the growth of membership has not been so rapid or overwhelming as Welch had predicted, the letters have not been in the proportion of "an avalanche" as he had requested. But in order to keep the members on the alert, they are required to fill in "Members' Monthly Memos," printed forms that detail all their actions and their observations on the Americanist fight.

The society's most successful efforts have not been on the national scale, but, as Alan F. Westin noted in *Commentary*, "on the soft underbelly of American democracy—those places where a minimum of pressure can often produce maximum terror and restrictive responses." These have resulted in secret boycotts, silent censorships and pressures on educators, newspapers and employers. In some areas the population has been supine and frightened by those Birch activities, but the case of the Birchers in Santa Barbara, California, showed that a crusading editor and a fearless populace could put the fundamentalists of the fanatic Right in their proper perspective.

Thomas M. Storke, 84-year-old editor and publisher of *The Santa Barbara News-Press*, told the story of the community's fight for the civil liberties that the Birchers were undermining. Storke, a strong Democrat, is frequently in disagreement with many of the conservative Republicans in his town and Montecito, nearby, known as the millionaires' colony. But he found that fanatic extremism is repugnant to most Americans. He wrote:

In 1960, it became apparent that organized effort was being put behind the activities of the ever-present radical reactionary extremists. A steady pattern of attack was emerging—against school officials, particularly in the adult-education field; against churchmen; against the United Nations; against university professors and administrators. Day after day, the mails brought literature vilifying the entire Supreme Court and calling particularly for the impeachment of the Chief Justice. Most of them came in envelopes bearing Robert Welch's now familiar battle cry: "This is a republic, not a democracy—let's keep it that way."

More and more, letters to the editor followed the familiar anti pattern. Anonymous telephone calls charging *Communist* became commonplace. Mailings to Protestant church members cast doubts on the loyalty and patriotism of their leaders. Santa Barbara was seeing the manifestations of organized activities, but most of our citizens did not know what was behind them—the John Birch Society.

I and my newspaper decided the people had a right to know about the Society that was trying to influence their thinking; just as all Americans have a right to form their own opinions from a free flow of information, and the right to promote their views in a legitimate way.

Storke assigned reporter Hans Engh to the story. Engh wrote it almost entirely in the words of the society, its founder and some of its local members. The story did not carry the impact Storke wanted. Cries of *smear* came from the Birchers and the pattern of attacks continued.

Storke then published the following front-page editorial:

The editor and publisher of The News-Press is in his 85th year. His entire life has been spent in this community. His memory takes him back many years and his reading even further. He lived when conditions were rugged. When West was West and men were men. He lived during periods when if a man or a group of men openly by word of mouth, or the printed word, called our President, or Vice President, our Secretary of State, the President's brother, members of the Supreme Court, and others at the head of our Government traitors, they were made to answer. Such slanders often called for a visit from a courageous and irate group which brought with them a barrel of tar and a few feathers. And such instances were particularly likely to occur if the slanderer came from New England. He lived when men were considered cowards when they hid behind their women's skirts and clothed their identity through anonymity.

The editorial, combined with the stories, suddenly brought an awakening among the citizens. Storke declared that "the results were amazing. Most remarkable was the support we got from the moderates, both liberal and conservative—the people in the middle who are rarely heard from. Community leaders who had been subjected to Birch attacks stood up and fought back, realizing that the newspaper and a broad segment of the public were behind them."

For his courage in acting swiftly against a subversive group, Storke was honored with the Lauterbach Award of the Nieman Foundation for Journalism at Harvard. The award was made at a banquet, and the scroll presented to him bore the citation:

"He has made his community his life-long concern; to guard its need from exploiters in his youth; to protect its character from destroyers in his age. He has demanded that public issues be discussed with decency and sanity."

Among the messages of congratulations was one from President Kennedy, who hailed Storke for his "enviable record as an independent editor and publisher . . . and your sturdy conviction and judgment." There were other messages of praise from Supreme Court Justice William O. Douglas and Ralph McGill, editor of *The Atlanta Constitution*. The award, named after the late Richard Lauterbach of *Time Magazine*, is presented annually to an American newsman for outstanding work in the defense of civil liberties.

Perhaps the best lesson the Birchers got in Santa Barbara

was losing their intense, bitter and vicious battle to destroy the UNICEF Halloween fund drive. After the usual campaign of vilification and innuendo against another "hidden group in the Communist conspiracy," the Birchers could not fail to note that the collection in Santa Barbara came to $6,000, against $4,300 the year before. Editor Storke concluded that "in the end, the only protection against such aberrations as the John Birch Society and such ridiculous leaders as Robert Welch lies in the informed good sense of the people. Air the ideas of the radical extremists, and you will find in a hurry, as we did in Santa Barbara, that the moderates are in control."

Storke said it was heartening to learn that other communities with similar Birch problems were reacting strongly. He has filled requests for more than 20,000 reprints of his editorial and stories from areas all over the nation.

"I have published my own daily paper in Santa Barbara for 61 years," he said. "During that time I have learned at least one lesson well—that a newspaper will not be listened to or win respect if it pussyfoots in stating its editorial beliefs. I have learned that you can't kill a rat with a feather duster."

One strong criticism against Welch and the Birch Society has been that in their frenzied battle against Communism they have become fellow-travelers of fringe groups that were anti-Negro and anti-Semitic. Welch has recommended such anti-Semitic persons and literature as Russell Maguire's *American Mercury*; Merwin K. Hart's *Economic Council Newsletter*, and Conde McGinley's *Common Sense*.

Hart, who has charged that "a conspiracy of Zionists and their confederates control America," was the leader of Chapter 26 of the Birch Society in Manhattan. A Congressional committee investigating lobbying described Hart's organization as one that "relies on ill-concealed anti-Semitism" to gain its objectives. McGinley, who is regarded as an openly anti-Semitic spokesman, embarrassed Welch with an endorsement in *Common Sense*. Welch has tried to shake himself loose from such associations and the hundreds of little hate groups scattered in tiny hamlets and musty clubrooms throughout the nation that want to embrace Birchism in their over-all campaigns against Jews, Mexicans, Puerto Ricans, meat eaters, Catholics and anything else they can be against.

Welch, however, makes the point that he has always appealed to all religions, has urged Jews to join the society and has warned that it is a basic "Communist tactic to stir up distrust and hatred between Jews and Gentiles, Catholics and Protestants, Negroes and Whites." He noted that the most vicious charges against him have come from "such notorious anti-Semitics as Lyrl Clark Van Hyning (*Women's Voice*) and Elizabeth Dilling (*the Dilling Bulletin*) on the grounds that my various committees and supporters are nothing but a bunch of 'Jews and Jew-kissers.'" Welch cites the names of prominent Jewish members such as Willi Schlamm, Julius Epstein, Morrie Ryskind, the late Alfred Kohlberg and Rabbi Max Merritt. He has been endorsed by the American Jewish League Against Communism, and he has been a consistent opponent of President Nasser of Egypt as aiding the Communists in gaining control of the Middle East.

Welch points with pride to a paragraph in an article about the Birch Society in *The Los Angeles Times* that said: "While some vague suspicions that the Society is anti-Semitic have been voiced, there is absolutely nothing in any of the society's available literature or in the utterances of its members to bear this out. The Anti-Defamation League of the B'nai B'rith has found no such evidence. . . ."

He devoted the major portion of an issue of the April, 1961, *Bulletin* to explaining his positions on Jews and other religions in their relationship with Communism.

When a Catholic or a Protestant or a Jew, or an American or a Frenchman or an Egyptian, becomes a Communist, he automatically discards all other loyalties. The Communists will permit no other God and no other flag than Communism, regardless of what temporary pretenses otherwise may be made by individual Communists to serve Communist needs. The new secret recruit in the Communist conspiracy may well pretend thereafter to be a better Catholic or Protestant or Jew, or a more patriotic American or Frenchman or Egyptian, than ever before, because the pose mightily helps his purpose. But it is one hundred percent lie and deception, no matter how skillfully it may be acted out. For either religion or nationality (or racial loyalty) is categorically contrary to, and specifically forbidden by, the very principles to which any real Communist must dedicate his body and his soul.

So I say to anybody who starts projecting general conclusions from the fact that he can name many Jews who are Communists: "Hold on a minute, my friend. Those people you are talking about are not even Jews. They may have been Jews once, and they may pretend to be today. It helps their dirty tactics tremendously. But Communism is so utterly incompatible with the Jewish religion, as it is with *any* religion, that these people are no longer any more Jews than was Karl Marx. And please remember, my friend, that Karl Marx, although himself of Jewish ancestry, became and remained, right on the basis of his own writings (including *World Without Jews*), probably the most vicious anti-Semite of all times. This is something these Communists posing as Jews never tell the real Jewish community.

There is only one real danger in the charge of anti-Semitism today, to the man who actually is *not* anti-Semitic. It is that the utter (and in some cases malicious) unfairness of the charge may cause him to react with anger against Jews in general, and then begin to let some of his feeling creep into his writings or his speeches. That brings on even more vitriolic attacks, with a few more straws to support them. And so the development continues until the man in question winds up actually becoming violently anti-Semitic. And he seldom realizes that this was the Communist game and purpose all along, of which the vast majority of Jews who innocently helped the Reds to implement it were as unaware and innocent as the ordinary Methodist who supports the National Council of Churches. And many an anti-Communist fighter of great promise in America has had his career ruined and his effectiveness destroyed by letting himself fall into that carefully prepared trap.

Undoubtedly I shall still be smeared unmercifully—even with this statement used as a basis—but I shall continue simply to say to my thousands of Jewish friends: "I wish you would pay more attention to how you are being used to help a cause in which you do not believe. But I shall remain your friend, no matter what happens, and I hope you will still remain friends of mine."

Under the firm guidance of Welch and his high lieutenants, the Birchers are required to regard themselves as completely dedicated to warning a complacent America against the dangers of Communism. The warning must be repeated on the highest intellectual level as decreed by the *Blue Book* (the official statement of the society's philosophy) and the regular instructions issued in the monthly *Bulletin*. Or, if the listener is unable to absorb the lofty philosophy, an earthy story about a mule is in order. It goes like this:

Farmer Bill: "Abe, you goldarned scoundrel, you told me that mule wasn't blind. But I hadn't hardly more than got him home and turned him loose when he walked headfirst right square into the side of my barn and durn near batted his brains out."

Farmer Abe: "Yeah, I know, Bill. He used to do it at my place. But I still told you the truth. That mule ain't blind. He just don't give a damn."

It is the task of the true Bircher to see that the Americans do "give a damn." The *Blue Book* charges that "one of our major problems today is the utter unwillingness of even the informed, conscrvativc anti-Communist in this country to face realities; to believe and act on the things their cold judgment tells them are true, but which their wishful thinking tells them to deny."

This superior attitude—that the Birchers know everything about Communist infiltration; the ordinary citizen is an innocent dupe—has encouraged forays into civil liberties in many small towns in the United States. Wherever they have occurred, responsible moderates have fought back, frequently with the aid of public officials. In California, Governor Edmund G. Brown asked Attorney General Stanley Mosk and his assistant, Howard H. Jewel, to submit a report on the society.

Light and serious by turns, the report said the "cadre of the John Birch Society seems to be formed primarily of wealthy business men, retired military officers and little old ladies in tennis shoes, bound together by an obsessive fear of Communism, a word which they define to include any ideas differing from their own even though these may differ more markedly from the ideas of Marx, Engels, Lenin and Khrushchev. In response to this fear they are willing to give up a large measure of the freedoms guaranteed them by the United States Constitution in favor of accepting the dictates of their founder. They seek by fair means or foul to force the rest of us to follow their example. They are pathetic."

Pointing out that, when the Birchers accuse our high officials of treason, they are doing the work of the Communists, the report shows that the society is "implacably opposed to the most effective of the free world's defenses against Communism—foreign aid, the United Nations, the North Atlantic Treaty Organization and increased military spending. Its opposition to these defenses is matched only by that of Khrushchev and Mao Tse-tung. Who is allied with whom?"

The report showed that domestically the society opposes civil rights, collective bargaining and the social gospel of religions. In the nations that they rule the Communists oppose these also.

The tactical forays against civil liberties were cited in

the report of a meeting sponsored by four local clubs (non-Birch) in the San Fernando Valley area. "Seventy to eighty Birch Society members invaded the meeting and broke into cheers and boos on signal," the report said. "They shouted the word *republic* whenever a speaker referred to democracy. The visitors insulted and interrupted the audience and speakers. The following day a similar group disrupted the peaceful meeting of a club in Encino. The Birch members were so abusive that it became necessary to call the police."

Attorney General Mosk expressed the view of most law-enforcement officers throughout the United States when he said:

"I am not officially passing on the merits or the demerits of the John Birch Society. Nor am I investigating the members. We in the attorney general's office are not Birch watchers. The Birchers have an equal right with the Prohibitionists, the Vegetarians, the Republicans, the Democrats, or, for that matter, with any Americans, acting singly or in group, to an expression of their views; and no official, no matter how highly placed, can say them nay. In America, preposterousness prevents the acceptance but not the expression of ideas. Should there be violations of law, as for example the disruption of public meetings, I am confident that local law-enforcement officers will know how to handle the situation.

"These are perilous times for America. The cold war goes on and a hot war, hot to the temperatures of fusion and fission, menaces the future. In such circumstances a patient, day-by-day analysis of facts is rendered difficult. Temptation is great to stop thinking, assign all evil to the enemy, arrogate all virtue to ourselves, and comfort ourselves in righteous hatred. The Birchers have succumbed to this temptation."

The report, informal as it was, struck its most forceful blow, however, when it concluded that "the entire Birch phenomenon is redolent with strong overtones of paranoia, with the Communists replacing the more conventional paranoid *they*. For the paranoid, life is a nightmare. Only he can see The Enemy. Only he understands the nature of the Peril. The more he acts upon his systematized delusions, the more he is cast out by his fellow-man for his oddness. This only serves to feed or confirm his dark suspicions and moves him to ever more bizarre beliefs."

Having been equated with the Communists, the Birchers also showed a parallel with the Nazis. Representative Henry S. Reuss, Democrat of Wisconsin, put into the Congressional Record a documentation of what he described as the "Seven Deadly Parallels." Reuss said he based his analysis on *Mein Kampf*, *The Politician* and the *Blue Book*.

"First, both detest the principles and institutions of democracy; second, both seek to destroy the established government, by fraud if possible, by force if necessary; third, both espouse the *Fuehrerprinzip*, whereby total control is exercised by the leader; fourth, both use front organizations to augment their strength with persons interested in limited parts of their program but who could not swallow the whole thing; fifth, both rely for their primary organization on a small, elite corps of zealots; sixth, both draw significant support from wealthy industrialists who should know better; and seventh, both profess militant anti-Communism, but they adopt with relish the dirty methods of the Communists."

Whether it is toward Communism or Nazism that the Birchers tend in their extremism, they are constantly confirming the charges made against them by moderates. In an open letter to Khrushchev, Welch wrote: "Your hands played the decisive unseen part in the run on American banks and their closing in 1933." The letter said it was the Communist-contrived recognition of the Soviets in 1933 that "saved them from financial collapse." He held that the "very idea of American foreign aid was dreamed up by Stalin. The trouble in the South over integration is Communist-contrived. The Communists have invented a phony civil-rights slogan to stir up bitterness and civil disorder leading gradually to a police-state rule by federal troops."

The Birchers charge that the Federal Reserve System is a realization of Point 5 of *The Communist Manifesto*, calling for the centralization of credit in the hands of the state. The doublethink or reversal philosophy, which tries to prove that what is ostensibly anti-Communist is really pro-Communist (except the Birchers), is carried on with continuing hysteria. Welch told his cohorts that "Communist influences are now in almost complete control of our Federal Government." Statistics, gathered by the Birchers, are made available in the monthly *Bulletin*, to prove all arguments.

Each year since 1958, Welch and his "board of experts" have published a "scoreboard" rating all the nations of the world according to the "present degree of Communist influence and control over the economic and political affairs" of the country. In 1958, the United States was rated as 20-40 per cent under Communist control; in 1959, the United States went up to 30-50 per cent; and in 1960, the figure climbed to 40-60 per cent. (At that pace, we will reach the 80-100 per cent mark in 1964.) England's rating went from 20-40 per cent in 1958 to 50-70 per cent in 1960. Israel is rated as 40-60 per cent controlled; Egypt 80-100 per cent.

Predictions of this type were calculated to increase the fears and frenzies of members of older right-wing groups, many of whom had also joined the Birchers. While Welch intends to build a unified organization to embrace all anti-Communist movements, he offers a patronizing salute to the others, stressing that "Americanists can work in several forums at once for the cause." He listed the other groups that he urged Birchers to support.

These were: the American Coalition of Patriotic Societies, the American Council of Christian Laymen, the Cardinal Mindszenty Foundation, the Catholic Freedom Foundation, the Christian Crusade, the Freedom Club (of Los Angeles), Freedom in Action (Houston), the Intercollegiate Society of Individualists, the Network of Patriotic Letter Writers (Pasadena), and We, The People! (Chicago). The Freedom Club of Reverend James Fifield arranged his Los Angeles rally, and the Sons of the American Revolution sponsored his Houston appearance.

When news of the Birch Society first reached the front pages there was a rush among right-winged public figures and genuine anti-Communists to investigate, join and support. But, as its excesses were made public, many exhibited reluctance to associate themselves with such a group. There was also, at first, fear to fight back, but after a period of timidity and caution the flood of denunciation became not only popular but almost mandatory.

The Right Reverend Horace W.B. Donegan, Bishop of the Protestant Episcopal Diocese of New York, gravely warned against the subversive activities of the Birch Society and other groups with equally dangerous programs. "They endeavor to reverse our American tradition of democratic opportunities and civil rights," he said, "to paralyze our Federal Government in its promotion of the general welfare and in other ways to turn back the clock in defiance of our national history and experience."

The United Presbyterian Church assailed right-wing extremists who disrupt its congregations with charges of Communist infiltration. In a letter, *Freedom of Pulpit and Pew*, adopted by the General Council of the Church, the 3,300,000 members were urged to avoid extremist tactics and, instead, combat Communism by strengthening their love for one another. The letter said in part: "With pseudo-evangelistic fervor and misguided zeal, some church members seek to convert Christians not to a firmer allegiance to Jesus Christ but to a campaign of anti-Communism based on a distrust of our free American institutions. In the name of preserving American freedom, they subvert it more by their reckless attacks on the churches, the press and constitutional government than the Communist conspiracy has been able to do."

Among the early supporters of the Birch Society were Richard Cardinal Cushing of Boston and Father Richard Ginder, editor of *The Priest* and associate editor of *Our Sunday Visitor*. But on March 1, 1962, the National Catholic Welfare Conference published an 80-page booklet attacking "extremists of the Right for fomenting a virulent form of disunity that is dangerously weakening the nation."

The National Catholic Welfare Conference is the central administrative body of Catholic bishops in the United States.

The Reverend John F. Cronin, who wrote the pamphlet, said it signalled the start of a "campaign for sanity" in meeting the Communist threat. He doubted the figures offered by Welch that about 40 per cent of the Birchers are Catholics, but conceded that quite a few Catholics belonged to the society, including some nuns and priests.

For those who ask: "What can I do to fight Communism?" Father Cronin suggests in his booklet:

> Devote all your strength and energy, in concert with your fellow-Americans, to building national unity and moral strength. Practice your religion and make it a vital force in your community. Even in dealing with moral evils, concentrate less on denunciation and more in giving leadership and example. Unite with your neighbors for racial justice and harmony. Do your part to make this a better and stronger nation and we shall not fear what the Communists plot and scheme against us.

Stressing that "many Americans are confused by the whole trend," Father Cronin declares that ordinary Americans are not extremists or crackpots. He pinpoints the fallacies of the Birch philosophy and issues a warning in the booklet. Speaking of the Birchers, he says in part:

> Their basic problem is frustration and even fear. They have seen the Soviet Union apparently gaining in its struggle to communize the world. Those who would have Americans concentrate on a minor threat of domestic subversion and ignore

subversion and Communist pressures in Europe, Asia, Africa and Latin America are misleading the American people. Whatever their motives, they are effectively aiding the Communist cause.

They are most effective when they can quote "experts" to bolster their cause.

There are three types of 'experts' whose credentials should be scrutinized with care. They are former agents of the F.B.I., former informants for the F.B.I., and persons who have had first-hand contact with the Communist party, either as members or victims.

Many of the more vocal anti-Communist groups have connected communism with social philosophies they find unpopular. Many, for example, use the argument expressed by a former high Government official in late 1961. It runs this way: liberalism (or the Fair Deal or the New Frontier) is the same as the welfare state. The welfare state is socialism. And the Communists say that they are Socialists. Hence, liberalism is communism.

Actually this statement is bad logic and worse history. As logic, it would make the encyclical of Pope John XXXIII, *Mater et Magistra* (*Christianity and Social Progress*), a defense of communism. The encyclical advocates or does not reprove many specific items rejected by extremist groups (the use of the income tax to equalize burdens, aid to underdeveloped nations, government action to smooth out economic change, social insurance, aid to agriculture, housing subsidies, etc.)

The violent and bitter struggle for racial equality in the United States has often prompted charges that Communists were behind these activities.

Actually, it is an amazing fact that the Communists have had such little success among the Negroes.

In fact, Negro leaders and the overwhelming majority of Negro people have rejected Communist influence and have insisted that they are true Americans. Whenever Communist influence is detected by the N.A.A.C.P. or C.O.R.E. it is promptly removed.

Protestant churches, especially the National Council of Churches, have also been a target for attack. Behind these attacks one usually finds opposition to the "social Gospel" or to alleged modernist trends in organized Protestantism.

Communist influence among the Protestant clergy today is virtually nonexistent.

Some anti-Communist sources are also anti-Semitic. These groups are small and have little influence except among bigots. The organized Jewish community in the United States is strongly opposed to Communism.

Groups opposed to the United Nations often use alleged Communist infiltration or even control as a weapon in attacking this organization.

Some of these opponents are basically isolationist and use the Communist charge as a handy weapon. Catholics who deny our international responsibilities do so in the face of repeated papal assertions of our moral obligation to seek world order, world prosperity and world peace.

The labor movement, and certain labor leaders, have also been the targets of special pleaders. Yet the C.I.O. wing of the labor movement expelled its Communist unions well before the general public became excited about the problem. Both wings have been working for years to fight for free labor unions, and against Communist unions, in Europe, Asia, Africa and Latin America.

Offenses charged to Communist infiltration also include fluoridation of water, promoting mental health and organized peddling of smut. Yet our organized dental profession supports fluoridation of water. The medical profession endorses sound mental-health programs. And organized pornography is a commercial venture, with no proven link to the Communist party.

Shortly after the booklet was issued, Archbishop William E. Cousins of Milwaukee, Episcopal Chairman of the Social Action Department of the National Catholic Welfare Conference, issued a statement pointing out that, while Father Cronin had written and published the booklet with the knowledge and consent of the department, "it should be understood, however, that no department of the N.C.W.C., through its Episcopal chairman or any of its staff, speaks for the body of the Bishops."

There was no doubt as to the effect of the booklet on intelligent, moderate Catholics, but Welch and his Birchers were still able to retain the hard-core fanatics. By this time Welch was still busy trying to explain his denunciation by that most red-blooded American of them all, J. Edgar Hoover of the Federal Bureau of Investigation. Without mentioning the society by name, Hoover, in an analysis prepared for the Senate Internal Security subcommittee, said:

"It is almost inevitable that, on many issues, the [Communist] party line will coincide with the position of many non-Communists. The danger of indiscriminately alleging that someone is a Communist merely because his views on a particular subject happen to parallel the official party position is obvious.

"The confusion which is thereby created helps the Communists by diffusing the forces of their opponents."

In an article in the *Journal* of the American Bar Association, Hoover also denounced the "self-styled experts on Communism [who] ply the highways of America giving erroneous, distorted information. This causes hysteria, false alarms and misplaced apprehension. . . . Emotional outbursts, extravagant name-calling, gross exaggerations hinder our efforts."

But the most ironic interpretation came from the Russians themselves, who stated that Welch and his Birchers were actively serving the Communist program. Under the date of April 4, 1961, the *Literary Gazette* of Moscow said:

The predictions of Lenin are materializing in the United States. Lenin said that the most ardent foes of Communism will eventually become frightened and suspicious of anybody who does not agree with them. In this manner these extremely nationalistic capitalists will actually work for the cause of Communism by eliminating some of the largest obstacles on the road toward a world-wide Communist way of life. Several years ago an American Senator by the name of McCarthy performed a great service for world Communism . . . by throwing suspicion of Communist affiliation on some very important personalities of the capitalist world. Instead of harming, he actually strengthened the Communist party in the United States. Now the Communist movement has gained unexpectedly a new supporter. His name is Robert Welch.

6. God and Country

In 1925, George Stuart Benson arrived in China as an eager
young missionary to do God's work for the Church of
Christ, a small but intense fundamentalist sect that denies
most modern doctrine, including the Darwinian theory of
evolution, and looks with suspicion at the 20th century.
Young Benson labored diligently among the heathen Chinese, attaining modest successes and noting with dismay
the travail and misery brought about by despotism and
totalitarianism.

He returned to America years later, determined to do
better for Americans what he had been able to do only
partly for the Chinese—educate them. He had been called
back to become president of Harding College, his alma
mater, nestled in the Ozark foothills at Searcy, Arkansas,
considered then and now typical of a back-water Bible
Belt campus. At the time the school was housed in two
modest buildings, had a student body of less than 200 and
lacked academic accreditation.

As he surveyed the social and economic conditions of his country in 1936, Benson, by this time the possessor of a doctorate, noted with some astonishment that labor unions had grown in size and number; that they were beginning to have a strong voice in government and that they were making the kinds of "arrogant" demands on industry that greatly resembled those of the Communist Party's platform. This came as a startling revelation to the man who had dealt only with coolies in his formative years—coolies who were always grateful for the tiniest gifts of simple food and shelter and who made no pretensions of seeking equality—coolies who allowed the missionaries to think for them.

Years later, he told Cabell Phillips of *The New York Times*: "I was shocked and saddened at the lack of understanding and appreciation that most Americans seemed to have for their country and their heritage. They seemed beaten by adversity, disillusioned with democracy, ready to give up a free-enterprise system that, even in the depths of the Depression, gave them a standard of living far beyond anything else in the world. They had lost their Christian convictions and their sense of moral purpose and were listening to all manner of false prophets. I had seen something like this in China, and I knew where this would lead, so I began talking about it to everyone who would listen."

Dr. Benson is a gentle, persuasive talker, whose zeal is muted by a determined serenity and a sincere kind of righteousness that is not offensive. During the late 1930s he talked to high-school groups, private gatherings and small organizations. It was suggested that he could reach more people if he wrote a column for a weekly newspaper in nearby Batesville. The column was so well received that Dr. Benson was invited to broadcast for 15 minutes a week over a radio station at Little Rock. Soon other newspapers were running his column and other radio stations were re-broadcasting his talks. His circle of friends and influence widened constantly, and it was especially gratifying to him that contributions were coming in to Harding College, which was his base of operations and his first love.

The period immediately after World War II gave Dr. Benson his great opportunity. Labor-management conflicts were erupting throughout the nation. Labor unions had grown so big that for a time it seemed that the ultimate struggle between big labor and big industry was at hand. The turmoil was frightening many citizens, expecially in the farm areas, where the last remnants of rugged individualism were still holding on. Dr. Benson pointed his philosophy toward extolling the virtues and wonders of free enterprise. He warned that the free-enterprise system would lose to a dangerous rival unless "American industry succeeds in re-selling our own people on the fundamentals of our own way of life."

This was a sound and patriotic position, and many industrialists listened with deep interest. His listeners in-cluded Alfred P. Sloan of General Motors, who felt that the message should be spread to the greatest number of people. Deciding that the most effective medium in 1949 was motion pictures, Sloan contributed $300,000 toward this end. Other industrialists followed Sloan's gesture with equally generous gifts, and Dr. Benson and his Harding College were launched as the official national institution to

teach Americanism as understood by the National Association of Manufacturers. With this kind of backing, the
educational program naturally adhered to the right of center
and, as *Newsweek* put it, "What M.I.T., is to engineering
and Harvard is to law, Harding College is to the Far Right."

The immediate, visible results of Dr. Benson's alliance
with big industry were on the campus of Harding College.
Today there are ten fine buildings and more are planned to
provide for an enrollment of more than 1,200. The school
has an endowment fund of more than $6,000,000 and
promises of greater things to come. In 1954, the school was
properly accredited—after it separated its extra-curricular
propaganda work from its academic program by creating
the National Education Program to carry on the N.A.M.
gospel in Americanism and anti-Communism. The N.E.P.
is a non-profit, tax-free educational agency with rent-free
offices in the Harding compound. Dr. Benson and several
of his colleagues serve both groups in official posts. The
N.E.P. has two full-time vice presidents not connected
with Harding College. They are Brigadier General William
P. Campbell, retired, formerly assistant chief of finance of
the Department of the Army, and Howard W. Bennett, a
former official of the General Electric Company. With a
staff of ten, these men issue a prodigious amount of propaganda that makes Harding College the leading disseminator
of anti-Communist literature with a little something thrown
in for the foes of social legislation. In his various capacities
and by several means, Dr. Benson has attacked the standard
peeves of the Far Right—centralized government, high
taxes, Federalized assistance programs of all kinds, reli-

gious and educational liberalism, foreign business competition and the monopoly power of organized labor.

Among the more important propaganda items issued regularly by the N.E.P. are:

Dr. Benson's weekly column, *Looking Ahead*, which is sent to more than 3,000 weekly newspapers (with no record of how many use it). A monthly reprint of one of these, under the title of *Listen Americans*, goes in bulk lots of 1,000 to business organizations.

The National Program Letter, issued to 50,000 subscribers at $1 a year.

A set of high-school study outlines on *American Citizenship Education*, sent free to any school requesting it.

There are 30 motion pictures that emphasize the advantages of the free-enterprise system and the perils of Socialism and Communism, and that are sold at prices ranging from $42.50 to $125 or may be obtained at a $5 rental. They are of a high professional quality and deliver their message in the smoothest manner and with high entertainment value.

Once a year the college conducts a seminar consisting of films, lectures and literature. It is generally attended by about 125 representatives of business, industry and civic and school organizations from almost all parts of the nation. The fees range from $80 to $140 and those attending the seminar are expected to go forth throughout the land and spread the economic and social "truths" as handed down by the leaders of the movement at Harding College.

Here is a typical list of the speakers, their backgrounds and their subjects as issued in the invitational brochure:

Keynoting the Forum, Dr. Benson will underscore the distinct advantages of the American system, showing why it is incompatible with Socialism and Communism. Upon reviewing briefly the history of the American Way, he will define its principles and examine its mechanisms of politics and economics. The basic institutions of the American community face threats from without by the apparent successes of the Soviet system and from within by apathy, ignorance and political demagoguery. He will toss out some challenges for the American community and suggest the basis of America's strength is in citizen-understanding and citizen-action in our civic, political and economic life. He will call for full mobilization of this nation's strength through education in citizenship.

Mr. Ed Hunter has been called the free world's most outstanding authority on "brain-washing," having introduced the word in his book, *Brain-washing*. Hunter will show how we can prevent our falling victims to the whole subtle strategy of brain-washing. He has testified before both the Senate Internal Security Sub-Committee and the House Un-American Activities Committee and proved that the anti-anti-Communist movement was initiated in Moscow and followed up with directives in America.

Dr. Clifton Ganus will present the basic structure of the American system by graphically building "block-by-block" the fundamentals that undergird our way of life and make possible the free American nation with its communities. If all American citizens understood clearly the advantages of our system, its basic principles and how it functions to produce freedom and economic well-being on a scale unmatched in history, the "isms" would not have much chance to take root here.

Mr. W. Cleon Skousen, field director of the American

Security Council, affirms that the West can win the conflict with atheistic Communism if American communities can be aroused to the realities of the struggle. His book, *The Naked Communist*, was called by a former assistant director of the F.B.I. "the most powerful book on the subject I have ever read." Skousen served more than 15 years with the F.B.I. in the area of internal subversion and has taught at Brigham Young University.

Elston Leonard, President of Fotovox Productions, Memphis, Tennessee, will give the behind-the-scenes story of the production of *Communism In Action*, the National Education Program's new 16-mm. sound motion picture. Mr. Leonard's experience in photography and audio-visual communication dates back more than 25 years, and includes personal contact with military and secret police during World War II when he served with the Army Pictorial Service in Berlin.

The Army's foremost authority and lecturer on brain-washing techniques, Lt. Col. William E. Mayer, of the Medical Corps, is a neuropsychiatrist who has served on extensive study projects in Korea and Japan, where he saw first hand the shocking results achieved by the Communists among GI's imprisoned in North Korea. As chief of psychiatry and neurology at the U. S. Naval Hospital at Yakosuka, Japan, he saw this hospital expand in 1950 from 80 to 5,000 beds.

A favorite American hero of both World Wars, Captain Eddie Rickenbacker is now Board Chairman of Eastern Airlines, but just as concerned as ever about preserving the American Way of Life for future generations. His dedication to American ideals and his religious faith carried him through many an adventure, and he says the fight to awaken our people to the dangers they face is the biggest battle of his life. The flying ace will maintain that the nation's conservatives must challenge the "liberal" political philosophies that tend to soften us for creeping socialism and further loss of freedoms.

Mr. Tom Anderson, editor and publisher of *Farm and Ranch*, is also known as one of the most quoted southern writers through his well-known column, "*Straight-Talk.*" "No writer," says Dean Manion, "can take that padding out of a stuffed political shirt any faster or more effectively than Tom Anderson." He is a most popular lecturer, especially in the conservative field.

Dr. Sylvester Petro has worked beside union members in steel mills, machine shops, and construction. He received law training, at the Universities of Chicago and Michigan, then followed six years of law practice and reporting in Chicago. He has been Professor of Law at New York University since 1950. Dr. Petro will outline to the Forum the critical role played by unit labor costs in our international competitive position.

Mr. Howard W. Bennett, a retired General Electric top executive who is nationally known for having designed the widely accepted economic education programs used throughout American business and industry; is now a Vice President of The National Education Program. He will summarize the National Education Program story and explain the unique audio visual educational materials available as "take home" tools.

During the Forum you will see numerous visual aids, during which some of the latest materials of the National Education Program will be previewed. The popular *Communist Encirclement*, already one of the most widely used educational tools in the country, is being updated and will be shown as Part One of a new series: *Communism In Action*. These and other materials will be available for conferees to see, evaluate, and take home.

A native of Boston, educated at Yale and University of California, Dr. Anthony Bouscaren is now professor of political science at Le Moyne College and a well known lecturer. Once a Marine Corps flyer, he has become an outstanding authority on Communism with five books to his credit. 1957-59 he served the House Un-American Activities Committee as consultant.

Dean Clarence E. Manion, Director of The Manion Forum, recognized as one of the great orators of our time, is a powerhouse of influence helping bring about renewed loyalty and patriotism in contemporary America. In discussing responsibility as the price each American has to pay for his freedoms, he will call upon a wide background of experience, including the deanship of the College of Law at Notre Dame.

Professor Perry Mason, a World War II Army Intelligence Officer, is now serving as an educational administrator. In their battle for the minds of men, the Communists have not overlooked the softening of youth right in the classroom. Education must remain a significant individual and community responsibility. He has authored six outlines widely used in our public and private schools.

Benton, Arkansas, has produced one of the country's greatest crusaders for American principles. She is Mrs. Carol Lippman, who confesses that until a few years ago she did not take the Communists seriously. After attending a Freedom Forum of The National Education Program, she began an intensive study of the Communist ideology. She has lectured widely, appeared several times on TV, and written extensively about what she has learned. This homemaker will stimulate conferees with her story of what one woman has done to fight the Communist conspiracy.

Dr. James D. Bales, professor of Christian Doctrine at Harding College, has an international reputation as a scholar of Marxian dialectics and has lectured at the National Taiwan University. Dr. Bales has given much attention to translating the jargon of Red ideology and has authored many books and articles; his latest is "Communism: Its Faith and Fallacies." He is now working with singer Pat Boone on a book about Communism for informing American youth.

Brigadier General W. P. Campbell, USA-Ret., received his education at V. M. I., the University of Arkansas, Columbia, Harvard, and is an honor alumnus of the select Industrial College of the Armed Forces. He was Assistant Military Attache in London when the U.S. entered World War II and soon became Finance Representative on General Eisenhower's ETO Staff. After World War II, the General was appointed advisor on Administration to the Peruvian Army, returned to the U.S. to become Chief of the Army Audit Agency and a member of the Army General Staff, and finally became The Assistant Chief of Finance, U. S. Army. Upon physical retirement, he joined The National Education Program.

CONFEREE COMMITTEE: Eight committees will be set up from the conferees for a brief new-idea study course to carry home. The question: What can various groups in organizational fields of church, civic, business, industry, labor, schools, housewives and teen-agers do to emphasize American principles to combat the Communist Conspiracy? Each committee, complete with chairman and advisor, will study a specific problem in time for a report to the full Forum on Friday.

As a hard-hitting finale, Dr. Benson will offer a résumé of opportunities for personal, local civic action. The theme and basic purpose of this forum are to instruct in regard to citizenship responsibility and instill a continuing desire for each of you to serve your communities. In fulfilling this purpose, you are insuring a more secure and greater America!

As in the other anti-Communist schools, the lecturers do not necessarily stick to their announced topics. Now and then, more often than not, they depart from the text to put forth their favorite phobias. Dr. Benson, for example, has charged that Harry Dexter White "did us serious damage when he stole our plates so Russia could print American money."

Captain Rickenbacker has urged the United States to sever relations with Russia, pull out of the United Nations and "finally recognize the war of total enmity to which our enemies are committed. For our honor and our undying souls, let's fight and die before the final enslavement. From all indications, we are heading toward an ultimate surrender. We must realize that a billion human beings are controlled today by two men, Khrushchev and Mao Tse-tung, and that we are encircled on three sides of the four by Communist-controlled peoples."

Rickenbacker had attacked the income tax as "Federal confiscation," and predicted that the tax will be repealed "because everybody hates it. Nobody can understand it. It cannot be enforced. Only the Communists want it. Take the government out of competition with private enterprise, and eliminate the billions of expenditures that are now going down a rathole annually. These billions are now being used to finance 700 large government-owned corporations that are split into 3,000 companies and 19,000 businesses, and each competes with every known phase of American private enterprise. This is done tax-free, rent-free and overhead-free."

As an alternative to the income tax, Rickenbacker urged a national lottery on the ground that Americans "are determined to gamble and risk their money on the wheel of fortune and lady luck. Why should all of the money derived from these illegal activities go to professional gamblers and racketeers when it could be used to support the Federal government? A national lottery would practically put out of business . . . those wishing to make a fast buck by devious methods, to say nothing of its effect in materially reducing juvenile delinquency. This would result in a great reduction of crime throughout the country and would save the taxpayers of the states, counties and cities billions of dollars now spent for law enforcement."

Rickenbacker tells his audiences that the ultimate battle will be between the "two irreconcilable views of government—liberal and conservative." He sees the conservatives "rising up across the land, finding new strength in their old convictions and making their voices heard. American liberalism is driving us into slavery, and with us everyone else in the world—for the death of liberty here will be the death of liberty around the world and the beginning of complete Communist tyranny for centuries."

To each of the forum speakers is assigned a special task in the general program of educating the listeners against Communism. Brigadier General Campbell's main job is to outline advances made by the Russians and point up the losses suffered by the United States since the beginning of the Cold War. It is an effective scare technique when delivered *staccato* and without at least some explanation. Here is part of the main delivery:

As proofs of our political ill health: The Suez Canal and China are both gone. Southeastern Asia is slipping fast.

France is in peril. The Arab World is playing footsie with the Commies. Since 1952, Soviet Russia has shot down twelve American planes, attacked five others with a loss of sixty-seven American lives, and not even one single apology. Iraq has dropped out of the Midde East defense system against Russia. Japan's Eisenhower mob explosion is still a smelly, festering sore. Okinawa is not a secure base. Korea is a shaky question mark. And even though we give Korea fifty-two per cent of her national budget, she had a big riot a short time ago because some students decided that we had too many strings on the many millions we give them annually. Turkey is having serious internal trouble. Africa is in turmoil.

In traditionally sedate London, one hundred thousand demonstrated recently in a Communist-oriented "ban-the-bomb" rally.

Anti-American leftists in Peru, Panama, Nicaragua, Ecuador, El Salvador, and Guatemala are causing grave anti-American unrest. Brazil has joined the neutralist bloc. Cuba's Communist microbe, Castro, has expropriated $2 billion of American property and says publicly that America is represented by a "scabby, lice-ridden eagle whose talons are torn by plunder." In Ecuador, our flag was dragged in the streets not long ago without even police interference. The New West Indies Federation has forced us to surrender five of the bases which we acquired in the 1945 destroyer deal. Khrushchev threatens us with missiles if we assert the Monroe Doctrine, and publicly calles us "thieves, cowards, lackeys, pirates, and mongrels." A few Communist students in little Uraguay forced the great U.S. to postpone the execution of a sex criminal. Rioters in Venezuela spit and threw filth on our Vice-President and his lovely wife and would have killed them if it hadn't been for the American Secret Service. And what does our Government do about these many insults? I am sorry to say, seemingly very little.

And in our own country, when the Committee was in San Francisco during May 1960, a large group of college students under the stimulus of trained Communist agitators defied the Congressional Committee on Un-American Activities and forced its members to a hasty adjournment through a back door under police protection, while mounted officers and motor cycle patrolmen held back the angry mob, and an American judge refused to convict the sixty-two "fellow-traveling" ring leaders of riot charges. So you see, it can happen here.

As with all extremist philosophies, Dr. Benson makes it clear that the moment of crisis is nearer than most people realize. The only way to save the country swiftly and surely is to press for the two main principles of the American way of life—Christian morality and the free enterprise economy. "These doctrines," he maintains, "are embedded in the Declaration of Independence and the Constitution. They have given this country the highest standard of living in the world. But our country and our way of life are under ceaseless attack by international Communism, since we are the last obstacle in its path of world conquest."

Having laid the noble foundation for his posture, Dr. Benson then issues the "commercial."

"The cutting edge of the Communist attack goes under the disarming guise of Socialism. The origin of modern Socialism is *The Communist Manifesto* of Karl Marx, and Socialism has advanced under such slogans as the 'welfare state,' 'public ownership,' 'government control,' and so forth.

Where outright Communism has not already triumphed as in Eastern Europe, China, parts of Asia and Cuba, it has achieved a strong foothold as in Latin America, India, France and Great Britain. The incubus of Socialism is particularly strong in the United States, where it is being actively propagated by a Communist fifth column. Thousands of Communists are infiltrated into our American institutions and are seeking to undermine our way of life."

Again, like most groups of the Far Right, the N.E.P. sees the peril of Communism as a prime domestic problem rather than an international one. "America can survive only if we make it impossible for the Communists to infiltrate us," Dr. Benson says. "This must be done by massive programs of economic and political information. It is a mistake to try to negotiate with the Russians on anything—disarmament, cultural exchange, Berlin or Laos. Foreign aid that is not coupled with anti-Communist military alliances is wasteful."

To reach the young people and the not too literate, the N.E.P. has issued a number of cartoon films, executed in the finest professional manner, that cajole, entertain, frighten and "inform" the viewers of what is the real truth behind everything. Here are the descriptions of some of these films as supplied by the N.E.P. copy writers:

> *Make Mine Freedom. Or, Curing Political Ills:* Dr. Utopia offers his patent medicine, 'Dr. Utopia's Ism,' for curing all political ills. Those who take it soon find themselves living under totalitarian government with troubles far worse than those they were trying to cure. Stresses the importance of preserving the free enterprise system and the American way of life.

Going Places—Profit Motive and Free Enterprise: A cleverly animated cartoon explaining the theory and workings of the profit motive and the capitalistic system of free enterprise in a highly simplified form. Freddy Fudso helped his mother make soap as a boy, became interested in improving the method, went into soap industry, was spurred on by profits to expand factory and distribution, and tried to establish a monopoly but was checked by a competitor and by legal restraints of government.

Meet King Joe—King of the World's Workers: King Joe is the average working man, who, with his high wages and short hours, is king of the world's workers. This is so because he has machines to help him with the hard, heavy work. As an individual he enjoys the benefits of the private-enterprise system. American workman is compared with the Chinese coolie in respect to pay and working conditions. Business and capitalism help Joe attain his status.

Why Play Leap Frog?—When Wages and Prices Rise: This shows the relationship between increased wages and increased prices. When wage increases are based on increased productivity, then purchasing power also increases, but if wage raises are made without a corresponding increase in production, then purchasing prices go even higher. Hence, prices and wages can play leapfrog.

Albert in Blunderland—Free America vs. the Police State: Through the medium of a dream, Albert, an American worker, is transported to Antrovia, a police state. Albert learns the real nature of a life in a police state with its political, economic and social impact. Albert's violations of some of the decrees of the Antrovian state result in his being sentenced by the minister of justice to be executed. The firing squad causes an awakening from the dream and helps him to crystallize his own thinking on the merits of our free system in America.

Living Under Economic Controls: This film deals with the efforts of a pitchman to correct a down-turn in the over-all economic life of a community called Eggville. Among the many plans set forth by the pitchman are wage and price controls, rationing, and other controls which eventually result in the closing of business establishments and the unemployment of much of the community's work force. The controls result in the strangulation of the economic life of the town.

Dear Uncle—Taxes, Taxes, Taxes: An illustration of the nature and incidence of the many taxes in America, especially of so-called 'hidden taxes' and income taxes. The film deals with the plight of the business man, the laborer and the farmer in meeting the tax bills levied on each by Uncle Sam to pay for a variety of government projects and services. According to Uncle Sam's statement, every individual must work three months each year to pay his share of government expenses with not one dime being paid on the national debt.

The Devil and John Q.: A discussion of the nature and dangers of inflation. In this film Lucifer joins forces with the international conspiracy of Communism in order to destroy the United States. The strategy recommended by Lucifer is for the Communists to keep trouble brewing in Asia and Europe and for the Devil to go to work on the United States from the inside. He is reasonably successful until John Q. Public sets out on crusade to explain the fallacies of sky-rocketing prices, unlimited credit and ever diminishing purchasing power.

America's story of productivity and plenty was well received, as attested to by thousands of letters. Metro-Goldwyn-Mayer distributed the films in more than 15,000 movie houses, where they were seen and absorbed, veiled propaganda and all, by 35,000,000 people who must have gotten the message that anyone against untrammelled free enterprise is a Communist, a Communist tool or an utter fool. Dr. Benson made certain to point out that the cartoons won highest awards at film festivals for their excellence in color techniques and story sequence.

The most openly controversial and most popular single film issued by the N.E.P. is *Communism on the Map*, which has been seen by some 15,000,000 persons in schools, service clubs, industrial plants and political forums all over the United States.

The film is a 45-minute technicolor masterpiece of professional perfection that gives the unhappy impression of America lying helplessly inside the massive snapping jaws of the world Communist conspiracy. Its essence depicts the subtle Communist approach and the brutality of its ultimate victory. The fate awaiting the United States is demonstrated by sequences showing the late General George Catlett Marshall representing the United States in China, "effecting a truce," the narrator says, "that aided the communizing of China."

There are sequences dealing with the Communist takeover of Czechoslovakia, which, the narrator stresses, was accomplished initially through the establishment of a coalition government; the student riots in San Francisco, "manipulated by Communist agents," a boastful Fidel Castro who displaced an anti-Communist government with America's assistance.

The film concluded with red and pinks suffusing the map of the world. All the important nations have been tinted and tainted except Switzerland, Spain and the United

States—in which at the fadeout rests a big question mark. It is a glorious conglomeration of misleading half-truths and platitudes shown in glowing, patriotic technicolor.

Persons of discernment and intelligence are quick to spot the subtle delivery of the film. Critics spoke out strongly against the picture, but the most effective attack came from 92 professors at the University of Washington after a showing on the campus. They wrote: "Having seen this film strip, we are shocked by its irresponsible mingling of fact and falsehood and by its gross distortion of historical events. As scholars concerned with the truth, we protest against this harmful and misleading propaganda."

But Dr. Benson was ready with his smooth reply. "If you are going to move Washington, to do the things it ought to do," he said, "you have got to move public opinion. My aim is to move public opinion at the grass roots in the direction of Godliness and patriotism."

7. Bless the ignorant

The Reverend Billy James Hargis is six feet tall, weighs 270 pounds, hates Communists and loves all others including Negroes, Catholics, Jews and the ignorant. Indeed, he loves the ignorant most of all because it is they, he believes, who are going to save the nation after he has educated them to recognize the true perils of the Red menace.

Founder and director of the Christian Crusade, with headquarters in Tulsa, Oklahoma, Hargis is a baby-faced, benign man who can put the thunder of revivalist fire and brimstone into his voice when he talks about Communism. He admits that his appeal is mostly on an emotional level and that he manipulates his listeners into a crusading Christian fervor when he denounces the Reds. But, he says, most people are uninformed and ignorant and the best way to reach them and make them aware of their holy duty is through the emotions.

He feels that this ignorance crosses popular party lines, thus giving him a practical political purpose for his Crusade,

"We are not trying to capture one political party or to create another," he explains. "We're trying to capture both political parties. The goal of such a coalition would be to help conservative legislation and candidates."

Hargis is certain that Goldwater can be President if the nation's conservatives put out the necessary effort. Then he reveals his entire program:

"My vision is of a coalition of effort. This is something conservatism has always lacked. There are more than 2,000 right-wing organizations, according to a poll made by a right-wing publishing company. Well, too often, they've gone off in 2,000 different directions. Some of these groups don't even know each other. Unfortunately, there has been some distrust among them. When you get trained in the Communist conspiracy, you tend to get cautious.

"On the other hand, the liberals have been consistent— always wrong. But consistent.

"The conservatives too often see a flag go by, get a patriotic feeling and write a letter. And too often that's all there is to it. My plan calls for getting the leaders of the major conservative groups to meet quarterly in Washington with conservative congressmen. There, they can formulate a united plan of action on how to rally support for conservative legislation and candidates. For every professional liberal or conservative there are 500 persons who are neither. That's who we've got to reach. That third group, the un-committed voters. I think they're conservative and will vote that way when they know what conservatism stands for. And the man who beats the sidewalks and rings the door-bells will get their support."

The practical application of Hargis' plan needs leaders,

and these are trained at a school where the tuition fee is $100 and the lecturers cover a wide range of subjects. Most of the students are ministers of the gospel, undergraduates, fanatics and some who are genuinely eager to learn about the Communist conspiracy "that everybody is talking about and nobody seems to be doing anything about."

The faculty includes big names in the anti-Communist movements, such as five regional leaders of the John Birch Society, two Congressmen, several former Communists and guests from other right-wing groups. The students, generally from Texas, Oklahoma, California, Arkansas, Florida, Kansas, Georgia, Louisana and, in small numbers, New York, Ohio and Pennsylvania, listen attentively, take notes and make tape recordings for use with their groups at home. The subject matter is standard extremist and irresponsible anti-Communism with attacks on the press, television, schools, churches, foreign aid, income tax and fluoridation.

Hargis begs his speakers to remain on the subject of anti-Communism, but occasionally a speaker, after making the solemn promise that he will conform, sneaks in his favorite obsession. One such embarrassment was foisted upon Hargis by R. Carter Pittman, a Dalton, Georgia, lawyer, who started off properly enough but suddenly switched to a two-hour dissertation to prove that Negroes are biologically and genetically inferior to whites.

"The Negro," Pittman told his audience solemnly and with studied conviction, "does have some superior attributes—in singing, dancing and athletics, but in culture, we know him to be inferior." Pittman, with a mannerism reminiscent of McCarthy, waved a book in front of his audience to "prove" his point. The book, *Who's Who in Colored America*, showed, he said, that the successful Negroes were light-skinned. "It takes white blood to make a Negro notable or into an aristocrat," he insisted.

Hargis called the speech deplorable and promised to be more cautious in selecting his speakers. He reiterated that he was not anti-Negro, but called for a right-wing boycott of goods or firms that "sponsor shows that make snide remarks and comments against Americanism."

Then, perhaps forgetting his sanctimonious promise, he said: "We're going to use the good old American weapon of boycott. If this stinking racial agitator, Martin Luther King, can use the boycott, we can, too."

Hargis has written several pamphlets to show that the Reverend Mr. King and other leaders of the National Association for the Advancement of Colored People have helped the Communist plot to take over the United States. He beamed approval when one of his favorite students, the Reverend Kenneth Ward, at 20 a pastor of the Rock Corner, Louisiana, Southern Baptist Church, said Pittman's remarks were detrimental to the school and the movement, especially when Pittman uttered the accepted double-talk: "I definitely feel that hate and prejudice are not a solution, but neither is integration."

At the most recent Hargis seminar, reporters from metropolitan newspapers mingled with the guests and students to seek atmosphere and opinions. Joseph Haas of the Chicago *Daily News* spoke to Mrs. Cam Rockwood, a widowed mother of four from Miami, who is a member of her local Birch Society chapter. "I find the seminar here informative and kind of frightening," she told him. "I mean, how close it is to the end unless people wake up in time." Eric Seastrand, 24, was sponsored at the seminar, all costs paid, by a woman of conservative views in his home town of Salinas, California. A student of political science at Hartness Junior College in Salinas, Seastrand said seriously: "I've heard the facts here and I think it is a fine educational program. How can you know what to believe in today without facts?"

Mrs. Medora Howard of Tulsa told an interviewer that "we have been daily sold down the river." Asked by whom, she said: "That's a good question. I think we're getting little by little to find out by whom and by what."

William Hugh Rutledge of Bossier City, Louisiana, who is executive director of the Citizens' Council of Louisiana, took special time from his other activities to describe the NAACP as subversive. He said his own group is dedicated to the defense of states' rights and fighting Communism. He accomplished a double assault when he said: "We saw that a lot of the directives of the NAACP came from Moscow. We have documented proof of the subversive nature of the NAACP."

Rutledge said he agreed with Pittman's "facts" on the inferiority of the Negroes, and added a "fact" of his own. "Heredity," he said, "is the determining factor of man's nature. I'll give you a classic example. Take that dance invented by a Negro [Chubby Checker]—the Twist. An anthropologist told me this was derivative of the brown primitive jungle mating urge." Mr. Rutledge did not elaborate why so many white people in the United States and Europe were giving in so easily to the "brown primitive jungle mating urge."

Hargis' seminars attract other fringers who loudly pound their drums with the confidence that a sympathetic audience is eager to listen. One such is the Reverend Ralph E. Wright, pastor of Corinth Baptist Church of Midland, Texas, who feels all America's problems will be solved if he will be permitted to select the books that should not be read. He distributed a leaflet, *Texans, What Do You Have in Your School Library?*

Among the books that are sending this country, its children and adults to perdition (Communism) were *Andersonville*, "the dirtiest thing I've ever seen"; George Orwell's *1984*; Aldous Huxley's *Brave New World*; John Steinbeck's *The Grapes of Wrath* and Thomas Wolfe's *Of Time and the River*. He said books written by authors who have been "cited as being or having been affiliated with Communist-front organizations" should also be banned. He included Theodore Dreiser and his *American Tragedy*; Sinclair Lewis, Upton Sinclair, Oliver LaFarge and his *Laughing Boy*, and William Saroyan and his *Human Comedy*. When he asked his listeners whether any of them had ever read any of these books, most replied in the negative, explaining that this "stuff was too heavy for them." But the Reverend Mr. Wright did not feel that he was wasting his time.

The noble profession of crusading for Christ and fighting the Communist menace has proved in the case of Hargis to be highly profitable. In the Crusade's sales rooms it is possible, nay, almost mandatory, to buy at prices from ten cents to five dollars, leaflets, pamphlets, long-playing recordings, books, tape recordings and pictures that deal with the Communist conspiracy or the fundamentalist religion. Among them are a recording of *Songs and Sayings of*

Billy James Hargis, $3.98; a taped speech by Robert Welch of the Birchers, $5; booklets entitled *Compilations of the Public Records* of—respectively—2,109 Methodist ministers, 42 per cent of the Unitarian clergymen, 450 rabbis, and 614 Presbyterian ministers. These booklets, selling at two to five dollars, purport to show the Communist or Communist-front affiliations of these men.

There are many others, but the grandest of all is a silver-framed photograph of Hargis smiling before a portrait of Jesus Christ while standing beside an American flag and holding a copy of the United States Constitution. All that for $6.50. Buyers are enthusiastic and sales are brisk, especially during seminar time.

The Crusade is, of course, a non-profit-making, religious corporation. Contributions are tax-deductible, and it has an income in excess of $1,500,000, with an infinite growth potential, as they say in Wall Street. The Crusade employs a staff of 50; Hargis, the only paid officer, gets the modest salary of $12,000 a year plus expenses. There are plans to move from the bulging headquarters into a new $500,000 building that will occupy a square block in Tulsa and include a "Liberty Museum." It has been made clear that the museum will be devoted to religion and American art. But one item will definitely occupy a prominent place—an enlarged version of Hargis, Christ, the Flag and the Constitution. Everything else will be built around it.

The expenses clause in Hargis' operation includes a $43,-000 home called the rectory; two cars and all his costs on the road. He travels about 50,000 miles a year in a $50,000 custom-built and equipped bus, air-conditioned and richly furnished. The bus is rented at $867 a month. All his earnings are given back to the Crusade, Hargis says. These amount to more than $200,000 a year from books, records and speaking fees. "All I own," Hargis declares, "is a $10,-000 equity on a 700-acre farm in Osage County which has a mortgage of $40,000. I haven't got any savings."

When Hargis goes on the road, his wife, Betty Jane, mother of five, stays home to care for the children, but leaves an admonition with the staff to keep an eye on the Reverend's diet. The bus has sleeping accommodations for five. It has fawn-colored carpeting and orange upholstery, a desk, a stainless steel kitchen and bathroom with shower, radio broadcasting facilities and a mobile telephone. The refrigerator is filled with lean meats and no sweets. An aide said that, if there is a sweet around, "Billy will find it. He's a connoissieur of food—the consumption of it."

Hargis' defense is that "I can't be on a diet and speak every night. I carry a tremendous schedule. I do 20 one-night stands a month, write articles for our monthly and weekly publications and record seven 15-minute and two half-hour radio shows a week. I broadcast for Mutual Network and 200 other stations and I also film a television show for 15 stations. My traveling is necessary for my crusade. I couldn't build a movement sitting in my office. I believe in personal contact. You've got to get out and shake hands. My creed is follow-up. When I get back from a tour I send letters to everyone who registered for one of our meetings. The bulk of the Crusade's contributions come from answers to radio, mail and personal appeals—and mostly in small amounts."

He admitted that some persons and organizations had

given and still give large amounts, but he refused to give names or specify sums. One of his better sources, he said, is bequests from estates of supporters.

While the income is impressive, the services rendered are also impressive, Hargis said. His purchased radio time costs $300,000; television, $30,000; printing, $200,000; salaries, $150,000; postage, $45,000; foreign missionary work, $5,000, and incidentals, more than $50,000. The organization is governed by a board of 46 advisers and endorsers including seven national councilors and a paid organizer of the John Birch Society who teaches the methods of Robert Welch. Hargis likes to stress the fact that his organization was formed before the Birch Society.

The Crusade has no dues-paying members, but there are more than 500,000 "supporters" who purchase material and respond "generously" to his appeals on the air. There is no financial conflict with the Birch Society, Hargis says, and there is "more than enough room for the two groups." He points out that the "Birch Society has accomplished much good on the local levels and Robert Welch is a man dedicated to the fight against Communism."

Hargis began his Crusade in 1948 while he was the pastor of the First Christian Church in Sallisaw, Oklahoma. He was 22 years old and received his "first shock when I discovered a Communist was a paid writer for a Disciples of Christ Sunday School publication." Hargis went to the president of the church's State Convention and asked him about this, he recalled. "He said to me: 'So what, some of my best friends are Communists,'" Hargis recounted. "He saw nothing wrong with Communism. This is the thing I couldn't take. I may have lacked a lot of other things, but I never lacked vision. I saw a need for people to learn of the Communist conspiracy."

He learned as he progressed. His only formal education was one and a half years at Ozark Bible College and then on-the-job training as an assistant pastor. He holds honorary degrees from Defender Seminary in Puerto Rico, Bob Jones University in Greenville, South Carolina, and Pike's Peak Seminary, a correspondence school in Colorado.

But, Hargis says, he had the "feel of the people." When he started to preach against Communism he noted the frustrated, the lonely, the confused and the angry people who stayed late to ask questions and be comforted. "They wanted to join something," he recalled. "They wanted to belong to some united group. They loved Jesus, but they also had a great fear. When I told them that this fear was Communism, it was like a revelation. They knew I was right, but they had never known before what that fear was. They felt better, stronger, more secure in the knowledge that at last they knew the real enemy that was threatening their homes and their lives. They came to me and I told them. That is why they are loyal followers and that is why they will always be with me to praise Christ and destroy Communism in the United States."

Hargis reports happily that "our movement is growing. We are no longer attracting only the old and retired, the lonesome people who just want to listen. We are finding more people in our audiences who are in their twenties and some of them are well educated. They are the ones we expect to act when the time comes. They are the ones who will work inside both parties to nominate more conservatives and write platforms that will not follow the dictates of the Communist plot against the United States. They are the big hope in this Crusade. And they came to us because they heard about us on the air and they read about us in the newspapers.

"This right-wing publicity hasn't hurt us a bit."

8. The Christian Crusade

Christ and Communism have become the irresistible combination that has aroused many lonesome, frightened and frustrated men and women from a hopeless torpor and made them flock to countless meeting halls where they can hear the one extolled and the other condemned. During the past few years it has become the most popular way of fighting the Communist conspiracy while propagating the fundamental religion. It is a clear contrast to the philosophies of the radical left groups of the 1920s and 1930s, which stressed atheism.

It is possible to get such education and hope from Dr. Fred C. Schwarz, who heads the Christian Anti-Communist Crusade. He conducts a school at which he says: "Logic and reason will tell us that a Communist dictator will rule America by 1973. Instinct and accumulated experience tell us that this is wrong, but the fact is that the Communists are conquering the world. The asset that we have to counterbalance this is our God."

If there is no quarrel with this statement, it is necessary

to go on to another that casts some doubt on the validity of Dr. Schwarz's logic. He "knows" that Nikita Khrushchev has already chosen San Francisco as headquarters of the Communist dictatorship. Schwarz has told his audiences that "the Mark Hopkins Hotel will make splendid offices in 1973 for Khrushchev [who will then be 79 years old]. And the people of San Francisco—those they don't dump in the bay—can be put in the Nevada desert, which is quite handy. The choice was made several years ago and was solidified when Khrushchev visited San Francisco during his tour of the United States. In fact, that's basically why he came to San Francisco."

He stated his credo and threw a real scare into the members of the Texas Legislature when, discussing *The Disease of Communism*, he said in part:

The tragedy of Communism is not merely that it murders; it makes murder a moral and a righteous act. When they deny the foundation of civilization, our Christian heritage; when they deny God, and His creative and redemptive love; they destroy the very foundations on which our individual value is built. In its place, the cold scientific morality of mathematical statistics emerges.

When the Communists have conquered the world, they will be left with the residual capitalist classes whom it is their duty to destroy. This is their proletarian moral duty.

A few years back the American Communist party would openly acknowledge that, having conquered this land, they would need to put to death one-third of the American people. This is not an act of punishment; neither is it an act of revenge—it is the fulfillment of Marxism-Leninism. An act whereby the surgeon takes the scalpel to cut away the diseased social tissue that the new and Communistically perfect may come to glorious flower.

We are living in an era of great danger, of vast peril; an era when the very future of our children is desperately menaced.

Communism is the literal fulfillment of Psalm XIV. "The fool hath said in his heart, There is no God. They are corrupt, they have done abominable works. There is none that doeth good." Emerging from this bottomless pit of Godless materialism, captivating by a glamourous vision of regenerate mankind, utilizing the perverted religious fervor of youth, and every scientific method, this torrent is sweeping the Earth, and Freedom stands menaced and home and children stand in mortal peril.

Schwarz, despite such statements, does not like to be equated with Robert Welch or the Birch Society. "There is always a temptation in fighting Communism to try to form a totalitarian organization modeled on Communism," he declared. "Certainly, these people, these dedicated anti-Communists, want a leader. They want to be led. They want me to lead them. But I won't do it. If Bob Welch wants to do it, he can; he's got a program of action and a lot of ready resolutions. But it's not my business." Then, to show that his and Welch's followers have much in common, Schwarz remarked that he sometimes gets the notion that "Welch follows me around the country signing up the people after I've worked them up."

As the repudiations of Welch's irresponsible statements increased, supporters of the extreme Right flocked to Dr. Schwarz. Early in his travels he found movie stars John Wayne, Linda Darnell and James Stewart among his fans and he managed to capitalize on that. He has also found aid among important business men, including Richard Amberg, publisher of S. I. Newhouse's St. Louis *Globe Democrat*, who sponsored the Crusade in that city, and C. D. Jackson, publisher of *Life*, who made a special trip to Los Angeles to ally himself with Schwarz after *Life* had published some unfavorable material.

Dr. Schwarz also got considerable financial support from the Richfield Oil Company and the corporate complex of Eversharp and Technicolor. Richfield gave commercial sponsorship on television in 35 western cities for a Schwarz-directed Hollywood Bowl rally, which he described as Hollywood's Answer to Communism. It was a three-hour show, which was brought to New York, where it was shown over WPIX, an independent television station owned by the right-wing tabloid *Daily News*, and the time was paid for by the Schick Safety Razor Company and the Technicolor Corporation. Appearing on the program with Dr. Schwarz were Jackson of *Life*; Senator Thomas J. Dodd, Democrat of Connecticut, and Representative Walter H. Judd, Republican of Minnesota. Also on the program was W. Cleon Skousen, who denounced the State Department for believing it could negotiate nuclear agreements with Russia, assailed Alger Hiss and called for a complete overhaul of the United Nations. Skousen, a former agent for the Federal Bureau of Investigation, is the author of *The Naked Communist*. Jack Gould, television critic of *The New York Times*, assailed the station for merely disclaiming any responsibility for the presentation.

"While the evil of Communism is something on which there can be agreement, the reason for its rise and, more particularly, how it should be combated must allow for more than one opinion," he said. The absence of any statement of policy by WPIX on the air was disturbing.

Ed Ettinger, vice president of Technicolor, said his company got "good will" out of its support of Dr. Schwarz and cited the fact that after a company-sponsored broadcast Richfield received in the mail many torn-up credit cards issued by *other* oil companies.

Ettinger became interested in the fight on Communism while he was a corporal at the end of World War II. He was in southern Germany when his outfit captured two German officers. He recalled that they had said to him: "You've won the war, but wait, some day it will be you fighting the Russians." After Ettinger got back to the United States these words "stuck in his craw." Then he heard Dr. Schwarz and was impressed enough to join the committee that started the first school. "I am not politically minded," Ettinger said. "I try to stick to the main problem—what Communism is and how it operates."

Eversharp and Technicolor, guided by Ettinger and Patrick Frawley, board chairman, planned the establishment of an American School Against Communism, where facts without fancies would be presented and extremism or irresponsible accusations would be scrupulously avoided. Schwarz was given help toward the establishment of a permanent site for the study of Communism. Ettinger and Frawley made it plain that they would be cautious in giving aid or lending their prestige to other groups. "We don't want to get involved with irresponsible amateurs," they insisted.

The implication that Schwarz was not an amateur and that he had the proper answer in educating people against the Red Menace did not take into consideration the fact that he had no control over many of the speakers who appeared on his platforms and spoke under his sponsorship.

In one embarrassing incident, Dr. Kenneth D. Wells, president of an extremist group called Freedom Foundations, was talking to his audience in the meeting hall when he noted that the television cameras were turned on him. He suddenly switched to the television audience and began to scream: "I want to talk to you Marxists and traitors out there. I know you're glued to your television screens. Get this, and get it straight. Get the message, comrades. This country's 20-year Rip Van Winkle sleep is over."

In a second incident, a retired Medal of Honor winner, Colonel Mitchell Paige, formerly of the United States Marines, solemnly told an audience that, while some people wanted to impeach Chief Justice Warren, hanging would be more deserved. The microphone was pulled away from him and he was taken backstage for a long talk. Then he was brought back and explained mournfully that "the feeling about hanging someone sometimes just comes over me."

Of course, Dr. Schwarz said, he regretted occurrences of this kind, but he never managed to explain why speakers of this type were able to get to his audiences. Other gems attributed to Schwarz guests are charges that fluoridation of drinking water is a plot to weaken American minds so they can become easy prey for Communist brain-washing; that the mental-health program is another brainwashing scheme favored by the Communist conspiracy, and that the stage, motion pictures, literature and comic books are intended to soften the minds of the nation by depraving them.

As proof of this, *Lady Chatterley's Lover* was described as a perfect masterpiece of Communist-inspired pornography.

Schwarz himself is a facile, smooth and convincing speaker with a bland approach and an enticing Australian accent that also combines cockney and remote Oxford. Those who hear him for the first time are startled, then enchanted, and, considering that he says what they want to hear, completely captivated.

Schwarz was born in Brisbane, Australia, in 1913. After attending the University of Queensland, he became a high school teacher of science and mathematics. He returned to the university to become a medical doctor. He also was a lay preacher for the Evangelical Baptist Church, and, as he recalls it, on one occasion, sometime in the 1940s, he got into an argument with an Australian Communist. Whether the Communist got the better of him in the debate, or whether he became aroused and curious, Schwarz does not remember. But he started to read all the Communist literature he could find and became so avid a student that his wife, who had been one of his pupils in high school, remarked: "I'm never alone with Fred. He always has Karl Marx along."

In those early days in Australia, Dr. Schwarz spread himself rather thin. He continued his medical practice, but also labored as a lay preacher, gave lectures against Communism and acted as a psychiatric adviser to a marriage guidance clinic. He impressed two visiting American Fundamentalist ministers, who asked him to come to the United States under the auspices of the American Council of Churches, a dissident minority splinter of the National Council of Churches. It was from this fundamentalist group that Robert Welch got his figures that there are 7,000 Communist ministers in the United States. Schwarz liked what he saw and did in the United States, and in 1953, "with ten dollars in my pocket and an idea in my head, I came back to start my Crusade."

He said he had the courage to approach the battle because "I was an evangelical Christian and the Communists are evangelical in another sense. I knew they intend to destroy what I stood for. I am not ashamed to say that I am a narrow-minded, Bible-believing Baptist. On that basis is built my Crusade."

He worked alone for a while, heartened by the responses he was getting from small groups in the Southwest and the Bible Belt. Because his support came from local groups that got together to sponsor him, Dr. Schwarz conceived the idea of a school. By the middle of 1961 he was the director of faculty of some eight such schools and their number was increasing rapidly.

A school in a community lasts about five days and includes the showing of films, lectures throughout the school day, which is generally 12 hours, and a closing banquet. There is time out for lunch and dinner, during which the students are encouraged to discuss among themselves what they have learned and how, at the end of the sessions, they can effectively fight Communism on the local level. The banquet is always a joyous, back-slapping affair in which everyone is satisfied that the knowledge of fighting Communism is well in hand.

Dr. Schwarz is always the chief lecturer, making as many as ten appearances during the five days—each lasting some 90 minutes. He is an adept performer, using the old sawdust trail techniques of warming up his audience with jokes and bright stories and humorous apologies for his Australian twang and his learned approach. He does not stand stiffly and talk down to his audience. Instead he uses a tall stool on which he perches or leans behind the microphone. He explains that this is in keeping with the school atmosphere. Whenever possible he uses a blackboard and pointer.

Having set the audience at ease with hints and assurances that this will not be "dull, dreary or dry," he proceeds into his weighty subjects with fervor and enthusiasm and keeps his listeners with him even if they don't understand half that he is saying. He deals with dialectical materialism; the significance of fronts and captive groups; Communist methods of physical and intellectual infiltration; the Communist philosophy on the proper use of violence; the emotional approach that entices millionaires, ministers and teachers into the Communist camp, and the general defense against any and all of these dangers.

No matter what subject he is discussing, Dr. Schwarz never departs from his central theme that his is a Christian Crusade dedicated to battling Communism's atheistic conspiracy against the Judeo-Christian civilization of the West. He tells his audience that he is an educator and a crusader, but at all times, and "first and foremost," he is a preacher and his approach is always evangelical. The atmosphere of the lecture hall maintains a revivalist flavor, which is the way Dr. Schwarz planned it to be. He insists that the single purpose of his school is education about Communism and that "anybody who suggests otherwise is either misinformed or dishonest."

When a speaker slips away from the main themes, as in the instance of retired Vice Admiral Walter G. Schindler, who attacked foreign aid as "stupid support for Communist-inclined countries," Dr. Schwarz glibly explains: "I take sole responsibility for picking the speakers, but none for what they say. I give them academic freedom." He makes the point that the "president of Harvard does not always have to agree with what his professors say."

It is with this attitude that Dr. Schwarz follows a cynical pattern of education in his Crusade. While he may stick faithfully to his single subject, other speakers invariably follow the accepted Birch Society line of denouncing the Administration, the Supreme Court, the schools, desegregation, the United Nations, labor unions and the intellectual community for being soft on Communism. Almost every fetish and every phobia of the extremists has been aired on the Schwarz platform. A typical lineup includes Herbert Philbrick, former undercover agent in the American Communist Party for the Federal Bureau of Investigation; Richard Ahrens, former counsel to the House Un-American Activities Committee; W. Cleon Skousen, an ex-FBI man, and Representative Walter Judd.

Dr. Schwarz's sanctimonious approach has gained for him solid and respectable support. In one of his first great Crusade sessions in St. Louis, the list of 60 sponsors included the names of leading manufacturers, merchants and bankers, the Mayor and the chief of police, the two United States Senators, and the two local directors of the Birch Society. Governor John M. Dalton of Missouri officially proclaimed the four-day session "anti-Communism week in Missouri."

In the manner of every good showman, Dr. Schwarz wants his listeners to have a good time. After they have heard Philbrick lecture on "Communism and Youth" or "Cybernetic Warfare," or Skousen on "Communism, Psychiatry and Crime," they might get a bit bored. At this point a speaker will come up with a terrifying atrocity story telling of the agonies of a Marine prisoner in Korea whose fingers were broken by a Communist captor because he would not renounce his faith in Christian democracy. It is a device, old and tried, that will shock any listener out of his lethargy and activate his adrenal glands to the point where he will forget the original purpose of his attention. A super-patriotic fervor is whipped up and, when the school is over, the audience will have had its "hate session." It was after one such session that a bright and eager young man told a reporter that he planned to set up an anti-Communist cell in his local chamber of commerce, and another vowed to start a Birch chapter in his college. Collectively, the listeners come away with the feeling that they have learned something that no one else knows, and, what's worse, that most people don't care about.

However, one young Protestant minister came away from the St. Louis school, and declared: "This thing has all the elements of a brain-washing except that the victims come here eager and ready to be brain-washed."

As the Christian Crusade marches on, Dr. Schwarz is gaining strength and power, and in some quarters he is expected to supplant Robert Welch and his Birchers as the leading exponent of the right wing. But Schwarz charges that it is "slander and misrepresentation to lump this group with the Birch Society." He frowns upon the recklessness and irresponsibility of some of the Birch literature, but does not hesitate to distribute a comic book designed for children that shows Communist guards shoving the aged and infirm into a concentration camp, Hitler style, to be destroyed as part of thc Communist plan to breed supermen by getting rid of the weak and the crippled. In fact, no government or responsible group had ever made such a charge.

Perhaps it is because of this hypocritical attitude that Dr. Schwarz is regarded as more dangerous than Welch or George Lincoln Rockwell, the leader of the American Nazi Party. He has the slickness and the intellectual agility to become a significant factor on the political scene. How long he can hide behind his sanctimonious smugness depends on how long he can control himself or his supporters.

Among his early critics was the San Francisco *Chronicle*, which rendered the opinion that Schwarz "is prescribing a dubious remedy for an epidemic that does not exist." The Alameda County Labor Council assigned two officials to attend an organization meeting called by Schwarz. They reported that those in attendance were not so much concerned with fighting Communism as they were with anti-labor propaganda and "right-to-work" schemes. Robert Ash of the council said Schwarz looked to him "like an old-time medicine man who could sell skunk-scented soap or anything else he wanted to the kind of people that attend his meetings."

Because of the respectable support he has received, the attacks against Schwarz and his Crusade have not achieved the frequency or the furore of those against the Birchers. Yet many moderates were perturbed over the broad acceptance his school received in St. Louis. They noted the large proportion of younger people, couples under forty and young men and women of college and high-school age at the sessions. There were also many small business men, salesmen, teachers, ministers and housewives, who listened eagerly and promised to carry "the word" back to their neighborhood communities. At that time the moderates took no specific action, other than to show their concern in letters to newspapers. But in California, where Schwarz was more active, a committee of leaders of the principal Protestant churches of Northern California condemned Schwarz, stating that the Crusade was part of the "radical right and wherever such schools have been held they were followed by a resurgence of attacks on churches, schools and councils of churches." Rabbi Sidney Akselrad, president of the Northern California Board of Rabbis, said: "I believe that the Crusade is not so much against Communism as it is against social reform and against liberalism of any kind."

Schwarz admitted he was pained by these charges, but he was even more pained by California's Attorney General Stanley Mosk, who described the Crusade as a "fly-by-night promotion." Mosk told the people of his state that "these promoters have not produced evidence that their so-called school is qualified as such under the laws of any city and county, or that any of the alleged instructors have teaching credentials issued by the state of California. Thus this is a promotion and not a school. It is a fly-by-night circus because it moves from city to city where the financial pickings are best."

Mosk's statement did significant damage in Oakland,

California, where a school had been scheduled with an expected attendance of more than 10,000. When the session opened with fewer than 400 and the total maximum attendance was estimated at no more than 2,500, Malcolm M. Champlin, a war veteran, lawyer and former agent of the Federal Bureau of Investigation, who was chairman of the committee that organized the sessions locally, blamed the low attendance on Mosk's statement and the belief that "the Communists are better organized—they have made greater strides—in the Bay area than in Southern California."

Dr. Schwarz boasts that he is prepared to accept and survive the attacks against him, but is saddened when such attacks reduce the attendance at his schools. A Crusade can run on enthusiasm and emotion, but what it needs most is money, and, in spite of early attacks against it, the Crusade has been making money. In 1962 Dr. Schwarz was expected to garner at least $1,000,000 for his Crusade. The year before, he told a meeting, he had collected a similar amount. One series of sessions in Southern California alone brought $200,000 to the Crusade.

He told a meeting in Briarcliff Manor, New York (one of his few in the East), that the Crusade is not an action group and is not formed on organizational lines, and its sole objective is education. Dues are $10 a year or $100 for a life membership, and, of course, all contributions are tax deductible. For his efforts, he said, he gets a $5,000 annual honorarium, and his wife, Lillian, gets $5,400 a year to manage his Australian office in Sydney. He sees her twice a year during his month-long visits home. He admits he doesn't have to touch the honorarium, since all his expenses are met by the Crusade. "It's practically clear," he said. "There aren't many who can save $5,000 a year." Just how much his expenses are is not known. Schwarz points out that he is a thrifty man who washes his own socks and dries them on hotel radiators, and has no need for worldly extravagances. A more outspoken follower feels that the money is not important to Schwarz. "But," he says, "suppose Schwarz is getting away with $100,000 a year—a man with his ability could make that much in business. Don't we pay Willie Mays $100,000 a year to catch fly balls? Isn't Dr. Schwarz at least of equal importance?"

The details of disbursements are vague, but Dr. Schwarz said that the Crusade is always making contributions to groups fighting Communism overseas. As an example, he cited a $48,000 gift for a rotary press in Kerala, India, to publish a daily newspaper fighting Communism. More than 200 persons are employed on the paper and and $10,000 went for a building to house the press.

Schwarz will continue to command attention as long as he continues to get the support of important civic leaders and industrialists. The Jones and Laughlin Steel Corporation, in one of its bulletins called *Planning for Disaster*, quotes him as saying that "the Soviets really aim at world conquest without war. If they can reduce the armament burden they will have more funds available for propaganda and political and economic warfare."

The company follows Schwarz' line by another quotation from the San Diego *Union:* "The importance of the cold war is not the physical threat, great as it may be. What is important is that this war can be won without a single shot. It could be won by the invisible softening-up attack where an entire nation is brain-washed into believing surrender is proper and regimentation is good."

It is obvious then that Dr. Schwarz must do his own counterwashing of his audiences' brains in order to beat the Soviets at their own nefarious game.

9. Man on horseback

Former Major General Edwin Anderson Walker is the man on horseback for the more respectable far Right. He is the torch bearer who would light up the nether world of Communism, and the wielder of the flaming sword that would destroy it. This is how he looks upon himself and this is how his followers look upon him. His favorite words in his crusade are those of another soldier—Major General Orvil A. Anderson—whom he quotes as saying: "Give me the order to do it and I can break up Russia's five A-bomb nests in a week. And when I went up to meet Christ . . . I think that I could explain to Him that I had saved civilization."

Walker is a serious, humorless professional soldier who never disobeyed an order except one—and this he could not help because, he explained, he is dedicated to the destruction of Communism. As a super-patriot he saw "the image of America in the Far East and the West distorted and grotesque . . . a picture of corruption, immorality and materialism. This kind of propaganda has hastened our retreat from victory through the years since the end of World War II."

His resignation from the Army, his entrance into Texas politics and his avowed profession to fight the Red Menace inside the United States and outside when the time came climaxed a military career as a combat soldier and a fair disciplinarian.

He was born in Center Point, Texas, on Nov. 10, 1909, and was graduated from West Point in 1931, ranking 229th in a class of 296. During the demilitarized 1930s, the six-foot-three-inch Walker was a hell-for-leather polo player and, as a dashing, handsome bachelor, the prize catch for hostesses. Although he played hard, he also worked hard to overcome the handicap of his class standing. Whenever possible he avoided desk jobs, and he was soon classified by his superiors as an officer who preferred action. He began as an artillery officer and was later assigned to Special Services, where he was required to be a paratrooper. When the time for his first test jump approached, he walked over to a sergeant and asked: "How do you put this thing on?" He got a fast five-minute course and climbed into the airplane. He jumped, landed safely and snapped to the test officer: "Check," a word he uses to conclude all conversations.

The Special Service Force, called Commandos, was trained for airborne, amphibious, mountain and ski operations. Walker led its Third Regiment in its first fighting at Kiska during the Aleutian campaign. Transferred to the campaign in Italy, he led his special force of Canadians and Americans in the fierce mountain fighting up the Italian peninsula and at the Anzio beachhead. His men made a surprise landing in August, 1944, on the Hyeres Islands off the French Riviera and captured a powerful German garrison that could have endangered the landings of the Seventh Army on the nearby mainland. Later his troops rejoined the main force for the dogged, bloody fighting up the Rhône Valley. As the war neared its end, Walker was detached from his Commandos and placed in charge of the 417th Infantry Regiment.

Back in the United States, he was forced into a desk job as assistant director of the combined arms department in the Field Artillery School at Fort Sill, Oklahoma, and then was placed in charge of the Greek Department at the Pentagon. It was during the Greek civil war that he apparently discovered the menace of communism first hand. He made an official visit to Greece and Turkey and began to discern the peril of Soviet militarism and propaganda.

It was in Korea that Walker suffered the traumatic experience that was to influence his later action. As commander of the Seventh Regiment of the Third Infantry Division and later senior adviser to the First Korean Corps, Walker found his worst fears confirmed. At Heartbreak Ridge he witnessed one of the most anguishing failures of American arms—the headlong retreat of American troops and the defection of our soldiers to the Communists. He wrote of his grief in a statement to the Senate Armed Services Committee: "I saw stalemate become the substitute for victory. The monument there became the prisoner-of-war cages. The 33,000 American dead and more than 100,-000 Koreans lost are the monument to the censorship of victory on the field of battle."

Close friends say that Walker became aware of internal

Communist subversion during his visits to Greece and Turkey, but the trigger was pulled in Korea. He began to brood over and read about what he called the frightening threat to his country's internal security. He was deeply moved and concerned and he could not understand why others, especially office holders and military leaders, did not share his convictions as strongly. He felt a depressing frustration over the lack of positive action.

He received additional indoctrination in 1955, when he was sent to Taiwan as military adviser to Generalissimo Chiang Kai-shek. Upon his return he said to friends: "We aren't doing enough." He pointed to his medals, the Silver Star and the Bronze Star with Oak Leaf Clusters, and remarked: "What good are they? The war is not over. It can never be over as long as subversion exists in America."

The incident at Little Rock in September, 1957, was destiny's way of proving that Walker was still the disciplined, obedient and loyal officer. Fanatical racists, among them John Kasper, were stirring old hatred and prejudices and causing the school integration riots that were damaging the reputation of the United States in all parts of the world. Eisenhower had tired of procrastination and ordered Walker with federal troops to keep the peace.

Walker obeyed. But before that, he says, "through appropriate military channels I repeatedly urged that responsibility be restored to the state's National Guard, whose loyalty neither I nor any other United States officer had reason to question." His suggestion was firmly rejected, and his men, bayonets at the ready, carried out their orders. But another incident took place that showed Walker, a Southerner, to be a man of firm integrity. He stood before an audience of white students as the nine Negro children neared the school and said:

"The 14th Amendment to the Constitution of the United States guarantees to all citizens the equal protection of the laws. Since the adoption of this amendment many states have provided separate schools for their children on the basis of color . . . Three years ago the Supreme Court of the United States determined that such laws . . . are invalid. What does this all mean to you students? You have often heard it said that the United States is a nation under law and not under men. This means that we are governed by laws, properly decided upon by duly constituted authority, and not by the decrees of one man or one class of men. Since this is true, it means that we are all subject to all the laws, whether we approve of them personally or not, and, as law-abiding citizens, have an obligation in conscience to obey them. There can be no exceptions; if it were not otherwise we would not be a strong nation but a mere unruly mob."

No one doubted the sincerity of the man, but this did not interfere with his continued strong feelings against Communism. In 1959, he joined the John Birch Society and tried to resign from the Army. His letter of resignation said in part: "The fifth-column conspiracy and influence in the United States minimize or nullify the effectiveness of my ideas and principles, military missions and objectives and the necessary American public spirit to support sons and soldiers. I have no further desire for military service at this time with this country and its influences on the home front."

The act was a deep emotional wrench for Walker, who had weighed his loyalties and his duty carefully. The resignation was turned down and Walker did not contest the decision. Stolidly he accepted the assignment as commander of the 24th Infantry Division in Europe with a clear plan for some unilateral action. One young officer in Germany later recalled that "before he (Walker) came everything we'd heard seemed to be good. Then after he arrived he gave a sort of opening address at a big party in the officers' club . . . pretty soon people began turning their heads and looking quizzically at each other. Afterward they asked each other: 'What's he talking about?' "

It became apparent soon enough what Walker was talking about. He was disseminating his own special brand of anti-Communism according to the gospel of Robert Welch and the rubric of the John Birch Society. Since it is not the practice for personnel to question or openly criticize the actions or statements of a commanding officer, Walker's attitude was for some time a matter of gossip. There was talk that, on the day when Edward R. Murrow was named head of the United States Information Agency, Walker almost had a tantrum. One highly placed aide told some fellow officers that "General Walker thought Harvard was the bad place, the factory where they made Communists. He sure was death on Harvard."

Then came the open action down the chain of command from the General's office to the barracks, the schools and even the women's clubs of 24th Division dependents. A list of recommended books included *The Life of John Birch*, written by Welch. Soldiers were asked to telephone Walker's office, Flak M813, so they could "determine your

Senator's or Congressman's record; to learn the truth about Communism so the cause of freedom can be revitalized." The voting records had been compiled by the far-Right Americans for Constitutional Action.

Some of his aides were worried. They pointed out to Walker that the Defense Department had supplied the division with an approved troop information program—a program that is in military parlance considered "ancillary duty" and assigned to a junior officer. He was reminded that historically and traditionally soldiers do not extend their activities into politically controversial areas.

Americans at home first read about the situation when the *Overseas Weekly*, with wide distribution among soldiers and their families in Germany, broke the story that Walker was using the Birch Society line in educating his men and their dependents. The story also quoted speeches by the General telling off-duty soldiers and their families that Harry Truman, Mrs. Roosevelt and Dean Acheson were "definitely pink." The newspaper, published in Frankfurt, said: "A special warfare office was established within the division to conduct a 'pro-Blue' campaign designed in General Walker's words to 'give a new and vital approach toward anti-Communism.'"

The newspaper further reported that Walker told his men that "Communism has infiltrated every institution in the United States in an attempt to overthrow our way of life." It said that in addition to the John Birch biography, the Birch Society's *Blue Book*, and magazine, *American Opinion*, were distributed to company and battery day rooms and put on sale on Army newsstands. The Division's official weekly paper, *Taro Leaf*, published articles from the magazine. The *Overseas Weekly* story said that Walker had addressed 200 members of a parent-teacher association connected with the Division and declared, among other things, that Walter Lippmann, the newspaper columnist, and Eric Sevareid of the Columbia Broadcasting System were said to be confirmed Communists.

The uproar at home was tremendous. Comparisons were made with the problems of France's President de Gaulle and his political generals. The unpardonable breach of the traditional rule that the American military must not mix in politics and the screams from the Right that Walker was being persecuted brought about swift action. President Kennedy ordered an inquiry, the report of which consisted of 900 pages and 12 volumes of testimony. It was determined that Walker had violated two Army regulations: one prohibiting officers from publicly attacking government officials, the other prohibiting officers from attempting to influence the way in which their troops vote. The General was then mildly admonished and assigned to Hawaii as assistant chief of staff for training and operations.

Walker steadfastly denied any improprieties, charging that he was the victim of censorship. He resigned from the Army, forfeiting more than $12,000 a year he would have received had he decided to retire. This, he said, left him free to pursue his crusade against the Red menace. This statement verified the comment made by Lieutenant General Frederic J. Brown, who investigated the charges against Walker. In an 80-page report, General Brown said: "I really believe Walker regards Welch as a novice in the field of anti-Communism . . . Walker is a sincere, deeply religious, patriotic soldier, dedicated to the nation and the Army. He is eccentric and is not only violently anti-Communist, but has for years been working at it with a passion . . ."

There was to be a sensational appearance by Walker before the Senate Armed Services Committee hearings on the muzzling of military leaders, but just before that Walker entered the Texas Democratic primary for the governorship against the advice of Senators Thurmond and Tower. Senator Stennis, chairman of the subcommittee that conducted the hearings, quietly muzzled Walker, who then issued a statement that said in part:

> There can be no co-existence on the battlefield.
> Our objective is not peace, but freedom. If we are vigilant and strong and willing and worthy to defend our liberty, peace will be at home with us. If the Soviet leaders are made to understand that we will fight, there will be no need to fight.
> The Communists are not fighters. They are not even accomplished intriguers. Much of their work is being done for them.
> Talk about co-existence is a concession to the timid and gullible.

Shortly afterward Walker proceeded to pursue his monomania to the extreme point on lecture platforms throughout the nation. Senators Goldwater and Tower declined to appear with him. He charged that Eisenhower was factually wrong when he said that extremists are always wrong. Walker said this could not "be justified by fact or tradition or our history or our heritage. I see extremists in all areas as basically being inspired by something that will bring us out of the world situation today."

Walker told a Dallas crowd that he had never seen an army with "less purpose and mission than the United States

Army." He said the United Nations was also responsible for his resignation because he felt that a United States soldier "took an oath for God and America—to defend her against all enemies. Today, our relation and subordination to the United Nations puts every man signing the oath under a double standard. We are sworn to defend America but have to abide by United Nations decisions. Under these conditions the oath becomes falsified and fictitious. I could no longer serve in uniform and be a collaborator with this release of our sovereignty to the United Nations."

He told 4,000 cheering residents of that enlightened city, Jackson, Mississippi, that the United Nations is immoral and that its late Secretary General Dag Hammarskjöld was a "Red Swede who took instructions from Moscow." He assailed the "Potomac pretenders who do not believe in the sovereignty and independence of the United States. They have undertaken to dissolve and divert it into a worldwide super-government of United Nations."

Walker cited the careers of Vice President Johnson and Senator Fulbright as examples of what he said was left-wingers' progress in converting American politicians. He called for a complete Congressional investigation of the perversion of national policy during the years after the war. He said bipartisan politics must be forgotten, and it would be "trifling with national security to save face for John F. Kennedy or Dwight Eisenhower, for Earl Warren or Hugo Black, for Lyndon Johnson or Richard Nixon."

He took Nixon to task in Los Angeles for his criticism of both the far Right and the far Left. "I'd hate to see someone start down the middle of one of your streets and see what happens," Walker said.

He told a Chicago audience that the North Atlantic Treaty Organization "now exists on Communist sufferance and will be liquidated on Communist signal." United States policy has "undermined the morale of NATO and participated in actions subversive thereto." He also attacked the American press and television for giving the Soviet space achievement so much attention that it amounted to an act of psychological warfare.

Walker insists he speaks for himself. "I am not being associated with any organization. I am not going to be a principal spokesman for anyone but Edwin A. Walker. I am a walking program . . . with ten years' experience. I am the program."

There are some on the far Right who feel that Walker, like Welch, has gone too far to be anything more than a sounding board. There are more, however, in the higher *échelons* of right-wing politics who firmly believe that Walker could very well become the "man on horseback."

There are many, respectable but irresponsible, who feel that a shooting war with Russia is not only inevitable but highly desirable as soon as possible. They are the ones who heed with eagerness the statement by Walker that "the military and not the civilian authorities should be in charge of nuclear weapons. The military should have full control of their weapons to include the responsibility for their planning and their use."

10. Sieg Heil!

By 1973, the President of the United States will be a member of the American Nazi Party. He will enjoy the support of a Senate and House made up of members of his party, and the governors and legislatures of the 50 states will be members of the same party. The President may well be George Lincoln Rockwell, who will be 55 years old and fully prepared to carry out a mandate from the people that he himself has drawn up. He expects to use only legal, constitutional means to win power because, he says, "the people will demand our services."

At present the American Nazi Party is small, very small, he admits. But it is a highly disciplined and hard cadre of dedicated true believers in "White Survival." One of the first acts of the 1973 government will be to establish a National Eugenics Commission to discourage "the unlimited breeding of the least desirable elements of our society, to sterilize those who are hopelessly insane or otherwise biologically dangerous to innocent, unborn children, and to encourage, with early-marriage subsidies and bonuses for childbirth, the reproduction of our best stock." This will also put a limit on the population explosion by keeping the "inferior races in their place."

Rockwell believes that "Adolf Hitler was the gift of an inscrutable Providence to a world on the brink of Jewish-Bolshevik catastrophe, and that only the blazing spirit of this heroic man can give us the strength and inspiration to rise, like the early Christians, from the depths of persecution and hatred, to bring to the world a new birth of radiant idealism, realistic peace, international order, and social justice for all men."

To this end, Rockwell proposes, when he becomes President of the United States, to "investigate, try and execute all Jews proved to have taken part in Marxist or Zionist plots." (On the Zionist part, the Communists fully agree with him.)

His master plan declares that "we shall immediately remove all disloyal Jews from positions where they can control non-Jewish thoughts or actions, particularly from the press, government, education, entertainment and courts. We shall expose the criminal nature of the hate-book of the Jews, the *Babylonian Talmud,* by wide publication of its actual vicious words of hate and extermination of all non-Jews. We shall cancel all debts owed to Jews by non-Jews, where there is evidence of unfair or immoral business methods or conspiracy. We shall establish an International Jewish Control Authority to carry out the above measures on a world-wide basis, to protect the rare honest Jews from the wrath of the people . . . and to make a long-term scientific study [to find] if the Jewish virus is a matter of environment, and can be eliminated by education and training, or if some other method must be developed to render Jews harmless to society. We shall establish an International Treason Tribunal to investigate, try and publicly hang, in front of the Capitol, all non-Jews who are convicted of having acted consciously as fronts for Jewish treason or subversion . . ."

The fate of the Negro has a fixed place in the program of the American Nazi Party: "We shall appropriate ten billion dollars a year, for five years, from the money now being wasted fighting over segregation, poured into foreign aid, and lost on Negro crime, and use the money to build a modern, industrial nation in Africa, complete with shopping centers, airlines, super-highways, cities and handsome suburbs, and everything else to make it the finest in the world; and then grant $10,000 to every Negro family of five or more migrating to the new land to help them build a home and establish a business. We believe that if this is done with ABSOLUTE SINCERITY, we can make up to our sorely oppressed 'second-class citizens' some of the injury and degradation we have heaped upon them, and help them to regain their self-respect and dignity as first-class citizens who will lead their own Continent out of its Darkness with their American know-how and our sincere and generous help. It is inconceivable that any significant number of Negroes will resist such an inspiring and historical opportunity. But no Negro will be FORCED to return to Africa. However, Negroes remaining in America will be rigidly segregated non-citizens."

It is noteworthy that Rockwell's over-simplification in the solution of the Negro problem bears a compelling similarity to the program put forth by the great Negro nationalists, Noble Drew Ali and Marcus Garvey, and currently by the strongly racist Black Muslims.

In Rockwell's perfect society, where definitions are precise and inflexible, citizenship will be reserved for the élite. "A proud privilege to be earned, not a right carelessly awarded simply by birth." To be a citizen, it is decreed, "an individual must have passed his 18th birthday, passed certain minimum tests of knowledge and ability to understand his government, be in the process of education or engaged in a productive enterprise, and be prepared to give his life in the defense of his Country and race. The conferring of citizenship shall be a major ceremony, to impress on all the precious privilege of membership in the greatest race and the greatest Nation ever to appear on the planet."

While its basic program is ultra-national, the American Nazi Party expects to be international in its scope. "The Marxist United Nations" will be abolished, the program states, and in its place will be an "organic Union of Free Enterprise National Socialist States, with a world police force to maintain order, and to bring the blessings of REAL peace, international responsibility and political sanity to the peoples of the earth." It is expected that Rockwell will find time to head this group also, or, at least, give it his personal supervision.

Being all things to all good (white) men, the Party adroitly swings over to the welfare state in its program of "Social Sanity." It proposes to enact laws that will "protect every honest working citizen from unforeseeable and ruinous catastrophes of all kinds; to assure him of education and training to the top level of his capacity, but ONLY to that level; to assure him of vital medical and hospital facilities by providing medical coupons usable with any physician and redeemed by the government; to protect him from 'easy-payment' debts by insuring that every working man can earn enough to live decently without mortgaging his future to do it; to make easily available to all citizens major recreation facilities such as vacation cruises, which give life zest and color, but which are presently dependent on wealth; to make all defense lawyers in criminal cases paid officers of the court, like the prosecutor, not paid by the accused, to remove the weight of money from the processes of justice involving the life or liberty of a citizen; and to protect the people from political and economic exploitation by any individual group."

The nation's economy will be refurbished, first with the abolition of the Federal Reserve Central Bank, which "was set up in violation of the Constitution." Rockwell's program "will cancel all illegal debt resulting from the semi-private issuance of INTEREST-BEARING money instead of genuine National Money, and issue all currency solely by the National Government, with no interest." Having cleared the field of the old, established system, the Party's fiscal Utopia proposes to "establish a National Economic Integrity Commission to eliminate speculation, the immoral gambling by idle men in the labor of others as a sole means of earning money. The Commission will insure that no able man is permitted to enjoy a lion's share of the luxury, products and services created by the labor of others without contributing his own share of goods and services by his own management, invention or labor. The mere delivery of some of the tokens called 'money' with absolutely no productive effort . . . is a fraud on society, disintegrates the character of such an individual, and destroys the honesty and strength of the society which permits it. No one man or group will be permitted to profit from ownership of any public necessity which constitutes a monopoly. All monopolies shall be owned by the whole people. We shall abolish the Marxist progressive income tax and estabish, in so far as possible, direct taxes on the users of schools, roads, etc., with a manufacturer's tax to finance the facilities needed by all the people."

Business, labor and the farmer will be "liberated" from bureaucratic controls and "free enterprise and free bargaining shall be allowed to produce the efficiency unobtainable before. We shall assist each group to form its own control councils, on a local basis, to maintain order and communication, and national industrial councils to establish policies of mutual benefit. The government will keep hands off all honest enterprises, labor and farmers so long as they do not coerce one another, take unfair advantage, or threaten the whole people, when compulsory arbitration will take place. As a temporary measure, to protect all honest producers during the necessarily chaotic conditions following removal of the present crazy patch-work of controls and subsidies, we shall guarantee all honest producers a decent level of family income, until genuine free enterprise can bring genuine and natural order to the economy."

As soon as he is firmly established in power, Rockwell says, he will "re-establish the actual functions of the Electoral College and return to the election of U. S. Senators by state legislatures." The pay of all government employees shall be directly dependent on their efficiency under applied modern business methods. "We shall ruthlessly eliminate the hordes of bureaucratic parasites who make our present government the most wasteful, inefficient and extravagant," he promises. "We shall call a constitutional convention to draw up amendments and strike out others to enable all the planned programs to be carried out, and to insure that never again can any subversive conspiracy bring this great Nation to the brink of extinction."

To this end, Rockwell expects the cooperation of an "honest free press," which he will assure by making it a "penitentiary offense for any medium of public information to consciously mislead the public by lies, misrepresentation, omissions, deletions, or by any other method whatsoever." To accomplish this, Rockwell will establish a National Free Opinion Network of Newspapers, TV, Radio, Books and Magazines. He will make these available upon petition by any group of 1,000 or more citizens for decent presentation of their views without cost, "subject, of course, to the penalties of conscious lying."

There is almost a touch of compassionate understanding of those human frailties, drinking and gambling, in Rockwell's attitude. "Since we recognize that it is utterly impossible to suppress entirely drinking and gambling in human society," he says, "we shall remove these two sources of much crime from the criminals and establish a generous national lottery, and place the sale of alcoholic beverages under a control board. At the same time we shall ruthlessly suppress all forms of vice such as prostitution, dope addiction, homosexuality, etc., which are NOT universal and necessary, and which cannot be tolerated in any form without breeding disintegration and disease. We shall deal ruthlessly and efficiently with habitual and natural criminals, and drive them permanently out of existence, instead of the present tearful dabbling with them as 'lost sheep.' At the same time we recognize that millions of our best people are driven, under the impossible chaos of our times, into situations where there is almost no escape from the pressures except some illegal action. We shall remove the pressures from these oppressed people with the rest of this program, and take every measure to help these basically good people, and restore them to a productive role in the community."

Rockwell's shock troops in the battle against crime will be drawn from rather unexpected quarters. He says: "We shall rescue most of the growing hordes of criminal teenagers by dealing with their need for aggression, action, danger and excitement realistically, by ending the nonsense of clubs and tea parties, and forming them into para-military volunteer Police Youth Auxiliaries, to patrol America's crime-ridden streets, and turn would-be muggers, etc., over to the regular authorities."

As these controlled teen-agers grow to maturity, he explains, they can be integrated into the larger concept of the Nazi organization, which will be the super-police force of the nation.

In Rockwell's society of strong, stern and dedicated men there is a definite place for women. Like the rest of his program, it appears inviting on first reading, but closer examination reveals that the fine rhetoric masks the mockery of words with which the absolutists catch their adherents. It is the mark of the demagogue that his words sound intellectual but their message is purely emotional. The author has quoted profusely from the platform of the American Nazi Party to demonstrate this point, but the best example

of all comes under the heading of *Family, Home, School.*
It is quoted in full:

We shall take vigorous measures to restore to women the
dignity and status they deserve as the creators of our citizens,
and to eliminate the terribly disruptive idea that being the
mother of a family is a job of any ignorant female, that she
is just a drudging 'housewife,' that a woman must do something MORE, something masculine, to prove that she is
'equal.'

We shall elevate Family Management to the status of a
genuine profession, which it should be, and establish Universities of Family Management to train women in a scientific and satisfying manner in pediatrics, gestation and birth,
family economics, nutrition, family culture, philosophy and
the arts, etc. Graduates will be granted degrees having the
same status as Law or Medical degrees, and honored by every
agency of the community for their accomplishment in the
fields of their natural abilities and needs. We assert that a
cultured, professional, thoroughly capable MOTHER is the
equal of any man on earth, and will see to it that society recog-
nizes that fact.

On the other hand, we shall eliminate from our civilization
the disruptive doctrines of a false 'equality'—meaning same-
ness with men—which is masculinizing and frustrating millions of our good women, breaking up our marriages, and
wrecking our sacred family life. We shall encourage the restoration of the father as master of the home, grant subsidies
where necessary to give the home and children a full-time
mother, and promote in every way the rebuilding of the home
and family as the very fountainhead of goodness in our people.

We shall put an end to the foolishness of 'progressive education,' and give our youth a disciplined ability to think and

understand, rather than 'social values,' which they should get in the home. We shall establish a physical-culture program with something more than desultory games and half-hearted calisthenics, to harden and steel our youth to maximum fitness and exuberant health.

Having arranged to shunt women back to the kitchen, to consign most Jews to the gas chamber, to regiment the United States economy, to fix the morals and mores of all Americans, and to send the Negroes back to Africa, Rockwell has only to carry out his program. It is reasonably safe to predict that he will not succeed, but in the years to come he will stir up furor, violence, bitterness and the consummate hatred and suspicion that are the chief assets of his movement. He is the undisputed heir to the organized ultra-nationalism, anti-Semitism and racism that were officially exported to the United States by Josef Goebbels, Hitler's dialolical propaganda minister, as the first beachhead in the conquest of America.

(While even Goebbels' techniques seem refined compared to the semi-literacy of Rockwell's *National Socialist Bulletin*, the American Nazi Party has propaganda instruments as unsubtle as any fantasy of a German Nazi peasant. The back cover of the *Bulletin* lists some of the material for sale. A "beautiful lithographed photo" of Adolf Hitler or of George Lincoln Rockwell is available for fifty cents. There is also a five-cent leaflet, *Niggers! You Too Can Be a Jew*; if this is insufficient, fifty cents will buy what is officially described as "Bundle of Hate Literature."

(The prize item in the inventory is toilet paper. A roll whose every sheet is imprinted with a six-pointed star costs fifty cents; for the same unit price one can also buy toilet paper similarly imprinted with a picture of Franklin D. Roosevelt, Bernard Baruch, Harry Golden or James Warner, a renegade Rockwellian now doing business in competition with the Commander. Such specials, however, must be ordered in minimum lots of 10 rolls of any individual design.)

While the basic decency of most Americans never wavered, Goebbels' propaganda touched certain sensitive areas of lunatic hatred that are always receptive to such ideas. America saw it first in the 1850s when a Protestant economy feared it was being threatened by the immigration of Roman Catholics. The Know-Nothing Party, which was anti-immigrant in general and anti-Catholic in particular, spread hysteria and bitterness for a few years, but collapsed after the election of 1856. In the ensuing years tiny islands of fear and hatred developed against Jews, labor, vivisection, meat eaters and drinkers of alcoholic beverages. Some were scorned out of existence, others managed to survive, and the Anti-Saloon League mustered enough support to shroud the United States in the horrors of Prohibition. These were the fanatical fringe who sought to dictate the lives of their fellows and whose great appeal was in the oversimplification of the solution to basic problems.

Some traitorous Germans in the United States formed the Friends of the New Germany shortly after Hitler came to power. The organization was discredited, died, and was reborn under the name of German-American Bund. Its propaganda spewed anti-Semitism under the disciplined guidance of Fritz Kuhn, who was convicted of theft in 1939. The Bund died a violent death and its former headquarters in Manhattan's Yorkville section is now a funeral parlor.

From the same miasma arose Father Charles E. Coughlin,

Detroit's "silver-throated priest," whose magazine, *Social Justice*, had a circulation of more than a million and whose radio audience was counted in the many millions. His weekly tirades against Wall Street and the Jews caused deep concern because in his early starts Coughlin was not classified with the fanatic fringe, but, when he rose in shrill hysteria and called Franklin Roosevelt "that great betrayer and liar," and repeatedly referred to him as the "anti-God," the Vatican showed sufficient concern to send Cardinal Pacelli, later Pope Pius XII, to America to dampen his ardor. It was not a swift or sudden action, but Coughlin gracefully faded from the scene. He retreated to Royal Oak, Michigan, where he taught school.

Gerald L. K. Smith, a former Baptist minister, rode the frenzy of isolationism in the middle and late thirties, boasted that he was a rabble-rouser and disclaimed direct anti-Semitism although his slogan was "Christ First in America." He still functions on the West Coast, issues a frankly anti-Semitic publication called *The Cross and the Flag*, and generally follows the old isolationist line with regular attacks on the United Nations and all international thinkers. His pretensions toward American Nazism, however, are frowned upon by Rockwell, who said in a broadcast over New York's WBAI that "Gerald L. K. Smith, in my opinion, is a political prostitute. He sells patriotism for money and he makes a lot of money. He takes in almost a half a million dollars a year. He lives in a mansion—he has two of them. He buys Ming vases and he takes the pennies of little starving people who give them to him in good faith, and he spends it on himself, which, I think, is vile."

There were others, like Joe McWilliams, who preached

violence, saw the light and withdrew to a quiet, non-political job near Chicago; William Dudley Pelley, a ranting extremist who nominated himself to be Fuehrer of the United States, rose and fell rather swiftly and died obscurely; Elizabeth Dilling, who fought taxes, "exposed" the *Talmud* and lapsed into inactivity; George Detheridge, who headed the Knights of the White Camelia, and Homer Loomis and his Columbians, who made some noises shortly after the war and then faded from the scene. These and other faceless frustrated men and women were the political ancestors of George Lincoln Rockwell.

What makes a Nazi? The biography of Rockwell will not supply the answer, unless the blame is laid to persistent failure. He was born in Bloomington, Illinois, on March 9, 1918, the son of "Old Doc" Rockwell, who was a popular stage and radio comedian in the twenties and thirties. Young George traveled about the country with his father and mother (later divorced). The older generation may remember Doc Rockwell, a top act on Broadway and in the first-rate theaters of the nation. He got a lot of laughs with a banana stalk that he used to demonstrate a little lecture on the human spine. When asked what he thought about his son's activities, Rockwell Senior said: "I've read a little about George's activities with the Nazis. I don't know how he hopes to get away with it, but he's just dumb enough to try. I will say this for my son. He's dynamic. He can accomplish a tremendous amount if he wants to. He was just as rabid a follower of Senator McCarthy." An aunt, Mrs. Roscoe H. Smyth, who lives near Rockwell Senior in Southport, Maine, said wistfully: "My nephew is a very brilliant young man, full of talent and genius—but we do wish he would find an interest in something else." A former friend (and Rockwell has many former friends) recalled his "fierce sense of superiority and a tendency to neat but oversimplified thinking. He was not a pleasant fellow . . . not one to get chummy with."

Young Rockwell was sent to prep school at Hebron Academy in Maine, where he showed an interest in drawing and painting. Later, at Brown University, he was art editor of *Sir Brown*, a campus magazine. He signed his work "Link Rockwell" and exhibited a continuing and consistent preoccupation with violence, death, cannibalism and bombings. If this was a normal outlet for exuberant youth, it was markedly different from the work of the other artists on the publication, who concerned themselves with the accepted undergraduate interests of girls, football, fraternities and dances.

He left Brown to enlist in the Navy during World War II. He became a pilot and by the time he was discharged he was a lieutenant commander. He returned to Maine, where he lived with his first wife and four children. The marriage ended in divorce. He was recalled to active duty during the Korean war and was assigned to duty in San Diego. Rockwell relates that during this tour he was introduced to the "Jewish menace" by a woman whose name he cannot recall. Whatever indoctrination the mystery woman gave him fell on fertile soil. He studied all the available anti-Semitic literature and declared that he was swiftly convinced that Communism was a Jewish plot to dominate the world and that only the "Nordic races were fit to rule."

At this time there came the "psychologically significant" incident in his life. The Navy transferred him to Iceland, where he read *Mein Kampf* and met his second wife, the former Thora Thors, a member of a prominent local family and the niece of Iceland's ambassador to the United States. They spent their honeymoon in Berchtesgaden, Hitler's former mountain retreat. He started to write articles against the Jews, which, he later admitted, "horrified my friends and my in-laws." Rockwell had four children with his second wife, who subsequently left him and returned with the children to Iceland.

He returned to the United States and started a nonpolitical magazine, *U.S. Lady*, for wives of service men. It failed. He next formed The American Federation of Conservative Organizations, which faded with a proposed publication, *The Conservative Times*. Rockwell was experiencing periods of depression and elation that were frustrating and confusing. He was a young man whose nervous system had a short fuse. He exploded easily and functioned best when he was hating.

At this time retired Rear Admiral John G. Crommelin was seeking the Democratic nomination for the Senate from Alabama on a platform of outright anti-Semitism and racial and religious hatred. Rockwell helped in that campaign at the suggestion of the infamous white-supremacist, John Kasper. Eventually he quarreled with both men and found himself again alone. There was no disagreement on philosophy. Rockwell simply could not operate as second in command. The *Fuehrer* complex was making itself his strongest motivation.

For some time he stumbled through the jungles of various hate organizations, seeking a place for himself, making many enemies and few friends, but gaining a reputation among the "moneyed" people that he was a "reliable hater" and could be depended upon to carry out any program with all the viciousness and bitterness that are the standards for this kind of operation. Rockwell, in his own words, found "several fat cats" who were willing to back his wild schemes for a Nazi America by 1973. He launched upon a series of sensation-rousing publicity stunts, such as picketing the White House and invading New York City with demands for "free speech." He was discharged by the Navy from the reserve; his sanity was questioned before a Washington court, and the American Legion's Washington Department asked for a Congressional investigation into his organization and its backers. Rockwell thrived on this. At one point he felt so powerful that he was able to denounce the late Senator McCarthy as "Jew-inspired." He told a radio interviewer that "Senator McCarthy would run farther away from me than anybody. His two chiefs of staff were two Jews—Roy Cohn and David Schine—and his adviser was George Sokolsky."

Rockwell and his Nazis are being fought by many established private organizations, such as the Anti-Defamation League of B'nai B'rith, but it is inevitable that the opposition contain at least one extremist group that will do battle with him on terms he can understand best. One of these is the American Anti-Nazi Mass Retaliation Party of Wayne, New Jersey, headed by Sidney Lansing, its "commander."

Lansing has prepared a plan of action in the event that "the Federal, state and local governments fail to deter Rockwell and his threats of extermination of the Jews." His organization, which, he admits, is numerically about as small as Rockwell's, is on the alert to meet violence with violence. If Rockwell were to speak in a community where the Anti-Nazis have strength, he says, "not a single Nazi wearing an armband with a swastika on it will leave the site of the rally alive."

Lansing's actual mode of operation illuminates the absurdity of extremist thinking. According to his plan, the moment Rockwell starts speaking, surrounded by swastika-displaying stalwarts, Lansing's men will move in and "a dark hood will be thrown over the head of each cop [guarding the meeting] so that he will not be able to identify any participants, and he will also be manacled from behind so that he will be unable to interfere with the operation. We will also disperse a large number of us to neutralize plain-clothes detectives in the crowd. Our men are instructed that no officers of the law are to be hurt. However, our men are told to exercise judgment that the whole effort must not fail because a cop or two was too difficult to handle. Others of our men will hold off Rockwell's Nazis while Rockwell himself is wrested from them by force. Rockwell will be beaten with our fists and his head will be smashed on the pavement repeatedly. And then he will be shot . . . not as a *coup de grâce* . . . but to make sure he is dead. And then the participants in this action will scatter and flee from the scene."

Mr. Lansing and Mr. Rockwell have much in common. All their problems seem one-dimensional on paper—and all their problems have simple and direct solutions.

11. The Minute Men

If the Far Right is a neurotic exaggeration of the unexpressed fears and frustrations of the ordinary middle-of-the-road citizen, then the Minutemen, a self-styled anti-Communist guerrilla force, is the psychotic, serio-comic exaggeration of the wildest dreams of the Far Right. Already repudiated by Senator Goldwater and all the other Rightists who could rush into print or to a microphone, the Minutemen are proceeding with a quiet and determined hysteria to prepare themselves for the day when the great Russian hordes invade America.

As a matter of unverifiable fact, the day is already at hand if one is to believe "Jack," the commander of a Minutemen group in Southern California. Large numbers of Chinese Communist troops are in Baja California and on the Mexican mainland. Hidden among the rugged Rockies in Canada is another force waiting to pounce upon an unsuspecting continent, and the infiltration is continuing every day, says "Jack."

"Jack" has to remain pseudonymous because exposure is dangerous for him. One of his predecessors was Troy Houghton, alias Troy Boyle, alias Troy Epick. He was picked up for failing to register as a sex offender. William Colley, another commander, was arrested for indecent exposure. This, says "Jack," is no reflection on the Minutemen. All organizations attract all kinds of people, who "are dedicated nevertheless." But when "Jack" got a lot of publicity in Drew Pearson's *Washington Merry-Go-Round*, he was glad that there was no other identification.

At a meeting near the campus of the University of California at Los Angeles, "Jack" said that not only are the Russians planning to invade the United States, but the United Nations also wants to occupy the country. "They'll have big smiling Swedes and Irish and Italians occupying us like in the Congo," he said. After revealing that his unit has a strength of 2,000 men, each with a rifle and 100 rounds of ammunition, and 800 with machine guns, "Jack" explained how the United States could be taken over.

There are many ways they could do it.

The UN is one of the ways. All the power that we're giving to the UN. Our counterintelligence units report large numbers of Chinese Communist troops in Baja California and on the Mexican mainland. There are several hundred thousand of these crack shock troops. Of course, if they invaded they wouldn't get very far, maybe only up to Long Beach. One American is worth ten Chinks.

But the UN would declare an act of overt aggression and would come in and occupy us. They'd do away with our Constitution and put in new laws—like their mental health laws. Do you know about mental health laws? They can arrest you and then they'll give you a shot that'll make you a schizo-phrenic and then they'll try you and find you insane.

There are lots of guys, sometimes whole blocks, who have bought rifles and plan to stand in the doorway and shoot. That's no good. When the man is killed, his wife'll still be ravaged [sic]—raped. And his property pillaged. We want to train people to survive.

The Congo shows what can happen. The UN crushed Tshombe. The UN can be anywhere in the world in a flash.

Read the UN Charter. That filthy rag! You know it was written by our friend, Alger Hiss, a convicted Communist. Did you know the California Constitution was changed and amended in line with the UN Charter? It used to be like the U. S. Constitution, with a few minor changes, Now it's like the UN Charter.

Did you know that you can be arrested for speaking against the UN on the street corner and you'll be tried by the world court? It's in the UN Charter. Read it!

Kennedy has more power than any other President has ever had. If he wants to do anything he just issues an executive order. Even if it's against the will of the people.

"Jack" hides behind his first name and goes on spewing irresponsible threats and charges to men and women who lap up every word as if it were the true Gospel. It may be possible to laugh him away, although the civilized world still shudders at the jokes it made about another man who survived the jokes to set the world on fire.

But not hiding behind a first name is Robert Bolivar De-Pugh, leader of a movement of "latter-day Minutemen," which he calls the strong arm of the Right. He is a somber young man, slender, with dark hair and dark eyes, funereal and Lincolnesque. He speaks with a disarming Missouri

twang-drawl, uses a college man's vocabulary for the soft-
sell and has a smooth and ready answer for any question
put to him.

A native of Independence, Missouri, where he was born
in 1924, he remarks casually that his father and Harry
Truman are good friends and, as a matter of record, one
of Truman's first jobs was working under the elder De-
Pugh in the city collector's office. Truman says he never
worked in that office and does not know the elder De-
Pugh. Young Robert will also mention his service in World
War II with the Signal Corps, the Coast Artillery, the Air
Force and civilian radar training at the University of Colorado. The Defense Department's only record of DePugh
shows one year, 1943-44, in the Coast Artillery at Fort
Monroe, Virginia, ending in a discharge for unknown reasons. The University of Colorado never offered a radar training course and has no record of DePugh.

DePugh grew up in Independence, where his father was
a sheriff's deputy for 30 years. Before the war he took
courses at the University of Missouri, Kansas State University and Washburn University in Topeka. After the war
he worked for drug firms and other companies in the Midwest and then started his own business, the Biolab Corporation of Norborne, Missouri, near his home town. He does
almost a half-million dollars a year making new drug products, including pills and compounds for animals and "geri-
atric hormones." He lives in a modest frame house with his
wife and five children, has no religious affiliation and is not
particularly popular among his 950 fellow-townspeople.

"Anybody who will take his family out on maneuvers and
carry empty guns around on their shoulders might do any-

thing," Mrs. Hazel Linville told Donald Janson of *The New York Times*. She, like other residents, was not happy that DePugh had put them on the map. All preferred to have the place remain the quiet agricultural village it was before DePugh became its most publicized citizen. "He's a very peculiar sort of fellow," said Earl Wheeler, owner of a hatchery. "I can't make out whether he's a genius or a screwball." Mrs. Lenora Fisher said the DePughs have "no intimate friends. They don't go to church or P.T.A. meetings." Noting that DePugh has not joined any local organizations and is seldom seen on the street, Robert Brown, operator of a gasoline station, said: "He kind of keeps to himself," and "he has not tried to sell the Minutemen idea to any of his fellow townsmen."

Mrs. DePugh, a loyal wife, said the town did not know of the existence of the Minutemen or the part played in the organization by her husband until newspapers and magazines began to tell the story. The Village of Norborne reacted coolly to the news. "People aren't speaking to us as they did before," she said sadly. "I'm looked on as if I were an oddity." But she had no doubt that her husband was working in a "worthy cause" and her neighbors might soon get used to the idea of having a "protector" in their midst. Her neighbors, however, prefer to look upon the matter as a joke—and hope it will never be more than a joke.

DePugh takes these rebuffs quietly and with sturdy optimism. "My group, which now consists of more than 30,000 throughout the nation, is more or less resigned to a Communist takeover of the United States either from within or without," he says. "If it comes tomorrow, we'll be ready tomorrow to go underground and begin fighting them. If it comes 100 years from now, our grandchildren and great-grandchildren will be ready."

He prides himself that he has created a casual formula for his organization that can include everyone—from rugged outdoorsmen interested in military maneuvers with guns to chairbound old gentlemen and ladies who can write letters to their Congressmen. There are no dues, no set program and no fixed table of organization. A general requirement is that the active men complete a series of 30 two-hour classes in guerrilla warfare and keep themselves fit to find and fight the enemy when he arrives.

"I now have a list of more than 10,000 individuals I can write letters to, encourage them to form their own groups, but I have little individual contact with them," DePugh explains. "I tell them I don't want to know your names. When the takeover comes, these names can be a matter of life and death. The Minutemen functioned for almost two years (beginning in 1959) without any publicity until the police raided a training exercise near Collinsville, Illinois. Now I've gotten so much publicity that, if the Communists take over, I'm a dead duck. That's the way I figure it. I must go on with the job."

After maintaining for a long time that he had no opinion about the Birch Society, whose extremist and hysterical ideology corresponds with that of the Minutemen, DePugh one day admitted that he had been a member for some time. He said that he was not fully familiar with the views of the Birchers; that his own organization was anti-Communist rather than political, and that publicity about his group and the Birchers had driven him into the Birch Society.

To coordinate the workings of the group, DePugh explained, some 500 members "chipped in" from $2 to $20 a month to the home chapter to cover the costs of printing manuals, postage and general mailings that run from $2,000 to $5,000 a month. The membership consists of a cross-section of the "American people," he said, "and some chapters are integrated." The movement is open to anyone not connected with a subversive organization and there are no restrictions as to sex, age, color or physical condition. There is no formal procedure for expelling members—"they are isolated from vital information and thereby ostracized." Even a felony record is no bar, provided a member "appears that now he is a good citizen and willing to bear arms for his country."

The movement is broken up into "cells" that are autonomous, functioning independently of one another, and, although the literature comes from the central organization, there are no binding oaths or single command to maintain a unified control. In the beginning local militiamen or vigilantes were formed with the anti-Communist idea as their goal and later affiliated loosely with the Minutemen. Thus regional groups have such different names as the Illinois Internal Security Force or the Loyal Order of Mountain Men in the San Diego, California, area. There are similar groups in Canada, Belgium, France and Holland. There is no chain of command either up or down and the essence of independent guerrilla warfare is thus maintained.

The training courses are generally similar, differing only according to the local topography. There are lessons in basic guerrilla warfare, survival and underground tactics, prepared from DePugh's library of 300 books on the subject as well as the experiences and knowledge of individual members. "A great deal of the training is done at night," he explains, "because that's when an underground must operate under realistic conditions. We study a great deal on night movements, infiltration of positions, scouting, the use of explosives, firearms and other infantry weapons, and hand-to-hand combat. Each group must learn every foot of its local terrain so if we have to shoot it out with the invading Communists we'll have the advantage of terrain over them. For instance, I have measured off the range of the land in my area so if I have to shoot it out, I won't have to rely on guesswork. I know every tree, every hillock and every hiding spot near where I live. No Communist invader can beat me or my men on our home grounds."

There are ten anonymous regional directors known to DePugh, but for the rest secrecy is maintained so that the members—"many of them doctors, lawyers, professional and business people from all walks of life—will not be embarrassed by public misunderstanding." The prime purpose of the secrecy is to prevent the Communists from building a file of principal enemies when they try to take over.

"I don't even know the members' names," DePugh says. "We have the name and address of the unit leader, and we don't mind if that is a pseudonym. You must remember that we are constantly building in secret. Our chapters have weapons caches and our larger weapons—machine guns, anti-tank guns and bazookas—are all properly registered with the government. We train with Russian weapons as well as American. Russian weapons are available from many sources—and if we have to use them we'll be familiar with them. Among our training handbooks we list 1,000 different sources of explosives for guerrilla warfare. If you put me out in the wilderness without any equipment except my bare hands, I could manufacture explosives."

Recruiting is done by word of mouth, mail and carefully placed classified advertisements. One handbill described the organization as "made up of loyal Americans dedicated to the preservation of both national and individual freedom. Help put real strength into civilian defense. Pledge yourself and your rifle to a Free America. For full details write Minutemen, 613 East Alton, Independence, Mo."

DePugh and his Minutemen are getting accustomed to adverse criticism couched in language that is less than dignified. Some leaders of the Birch Society have called them "idiots and screwballs." Col. Ralph Redborn, Civil Defense Director of Arizona, said: "We don't want any unorganized mobs in Arizona." Melville Stark, Civil Defense director of Riverside County in California, said: "Such groups could be very dangerous if controlled by the wrong people. There is no reason for them to be independent of established public agencies."

The Federal Bureau of Investigation has looked into the Minutemen organization and has shown concern over one paragraph in the group's literature that says: "We must investigate by means of our own secret membership the possible infiltration of Communist sympathizers into American organizations of government, business, labor, religion or education."

Such unilateral police work is not regarded as unhealthy or un-American by DePugh. "We're certainly not trying to compete with the Federal Bureau of Investigation or the Central Intelligence Agency," he says. "But on a local basis we feel we're in a better position to know and to investigate our friends and neighbors better than anybody else. If there is a potential enemy among us, we want to be the first to know and uncover him."

As justification for his organization, DePugh likes to cite President Kennedy's speech in which he said: "We need a nation of Minute Men; citizens who are not only prepared to take up arms, but citizens who regard the preservation of freedom as a basic purpose of their daily life."

The quotation was naturally out of context and interpreted to suit the requirements of the extremists, but DePugh must have recoiled when the President chose Southern California to launch a direct attack on Far-Right and lunatic fringe political movements that have sprouted like toadstools out of the tensions of the cold war.

Without mentioning the Birch Society or the Minutemen or any other group or school of the Far Right by name, President Kennedy made clear the position of the American people when he said:

> . . . The discordant voices of extremism are heard once again in the land. Men who are unwilling to face up to the danger from without are convinced that the real danger comes from within. They look suspiciously at their neighbors and their leaders. They call for a man on horseback because they do not trust the people. They find treason in our finest churches, in our highest court and even in the treatment of our water. Let us not heed these councils of fear and suspicion. Let us concentrate more on keeping enemy bombers and missiles away from our shores, and concentrate less on keeping neighbors away from our shelters. Let us devote less energy to organized armed bands of civilian guerrillas that are

more likely to supply local vigilantes than national vigilance. Let our patriotism be reflected in the creation of confidence, rather than crusades of suspicion.

DePugh noted this criticism with the laconic explanation that "a lot of people in this country are Communists without knowing it themselves." It is his fixed intention to protect these people against themselves and he hopes that, when the Communist invasion is defeated by the guerrilla tactics of the Minutemen, the country will be grateful. In the meantime he shows open contempt for the existing civil defense organization, Federal or local, charging that it is a device to reward political hacks with easy jobs. He is not quite certain about his policy on bomb shelters, feeling that they may have some use in keeping families together but offer no protection against the nerve gas and bacteriological warfare that the Russians are sure to wage against this country.

DePugh may be soft-spoken and almost self-effacing in friendly conversation; he may give the superficial impression that his approach is casual, but all this is quickly exposed as mere stagecraft when he issues this sort of statement:

"We must be willing to continue the fight for liberty even though we no longer have the legal support of established authority. We must prepare ourselves to take any action—no matter how brutal that may be—required to renew the protection of the United States Constitution for future generations."

So far, DePugh has been the only spokesman for the Minutemen who has received some recognition. While constantly denying that he wants to be a leader, or the "man on horseback" to protect the United States against the great enemy, DePugh continues to build his organization with an intensity that should not be ignored.

He does depart a little from the desperate pessimism of all present extremist groups, to the effect that the Communist assault is already in being and action should be taken swiftly and ruthlessly. When pressed in an interview on how certain he is about the present danger, he answers with a little hedge. "We hope we are wrong about the Communist takeover," he says. "If we are, the time in learning guerrilla tactics and the handling of weapons won't be wasted. It is a healthful pursuit, stimulating and a fine hobby."

12. White is for purity

The White Supremacists are aware that they are fighting a losing battle. Even though emotion and tradition rule their reasoning and dominate their actions, they must know that time is on the side of the Negro. But they know also that time is plentiful and their retreat can be extended for many years. This, then, is the objective of the present generation of White Supremacists—to stave off total integration as long as possible.

The struggle began right after the Civil War and has been constant, with varying degrees of intensity, ever since. The stories of the Ku Klux Klan, the Night Riders and other groups dedicated to "keeping the Negro in his place" are part of the agonizing folklore of America. Slowly but steadily the Negro emerged from the cotton plantations and began to gain an education of sorts under the "separate but equal" ruling of an earlier Supreme Court. He enjoyed greater freedom in the North, but still lived in ghettos that created segregated schools. For years, the White Supremacists felt that they had at least retarded the progress of the

Negro on his path to equality. During periods of prosperity, it was noted by the Fair Employment Practices Commission, there was greater tolerance of the Negro in all sections of the United States, but, when jobs became scarce during periods of recession, the hatred was revived. Economics, the F.E.P.C. maintained, was one of several clues to better race relations.

During these years there were incidents—lynchings, riots, the burning of crosses—but somehow they were written off as part of the American scene, to be regretted by moderates and disposed of by noble-sounding resolutions. The Negroes bore this travail with deep resentment and increased determination to intensify their struggle.

Such was the climate of the nation when on May 17, 1954, the United States Supreme Court unanimously declared that racial segregation of pupils in public schools was unconstitutional. The people in the North were startled at first, but smugly pointed out that in most northern states the decision was merely academic; that there really was no segregation in schools other than the kind that was accidental because of the location of "Negro residential sections." The people in the South were stunned, yet the moderates there began to study means of following the court's order of integration with "deliberate speed."

But the White Supremacists had no such intentions. Less than two months after the decision, the first White Citizens' Council was formed in Indianola, Mississippi, the seat of Sunflower County. Its formation was announced during the regular session of the Legislature at Jackson and was greeted with cheers. The people of Mississippi and the rest of the South were informed that "fourteen men met and counseled together on the terrible crisis precipitated by the United States Supreme Court in its Black Monday decision. For the first time in American history, racial segregation, the way of life regulating the daily activities of tens of millions of American citizens, black and white, in a well known pattern of familiar and satisfactory conduct, has been declared illegal. Despite the long-range dangers to our constitutional safeguards apparent to many men, North, South, East and West, in legislation by judicial fiat, the immediate and pressing danger to men and women in Mississippi and the rest of the South is the potential flood of Negro invasion into our schools, parks, swimming pools, restaurants, hotels, trains, buses, into our very neighborhoods and homes, and into public office. To thoughtful men, concerned for the safety and welfare of their families and children's children, the prospect opened up by this politically inspired decree appears utterly unthinkable."

The Klan, long discredited, appeared only in the background as other groups began to form, such as the States' Rights Council, the Society to Maintain Segregation, the Southern Gentlemen, and local units of varied names with but a single purpose. They included the stable, influential citizens of the community as well as the local "white trash" and hoodlum elements. In October, 1954, the Association of Citizens' Councils was organized at Winona, Mississippi. At that time the Association declared that "the supreme power in the government of men has always been public opinion. Public sentiment is the law. Only through grass-roots organization could public sentiment be mobilized and expressed."

Any comparison with the Klan was swiftly discouraged

by the Councils. It was pointed out that there was nothing secret in the operations of the Councils; there were no uniforms, no violence and no burning of crosses. Instead, the Councils insisted, the emphasis was on education and the use of public opinion. Speakers were made available to carry the message of segregation to willing listeners in the South or the North. A steady stream of printed information on "the nature of the crisis" was made available for the asking. Among the earliest pamphlets distributed was an address by Judge Tom P. Brady, a past vice president of the Mississippi Bar Association, then serving a second term as Circuit Judge of the 14th Judicial District.

Judge Brady declared unequivocally that:

Ninety-eight per cent of both races prefer segregation. Integration is urged by the N.A.A.C.P., a few Southern mulattoes, Northern Communist-front organizations and left-wing labor groups who would use the unsuspecting Negro as their tool. I want you to distinctly understand that the South does not hate the Negro. I dare say you know little, if anything, about the true Southern Negro. Among the finest characters I have ever known are Negroes. There is a great deal of genuine affection and understanding between the races. We have lived harmoniously together with a minimum of violence and bloodshed. We have nurtured the Negro, taught him, provided for him, educated him and endeavored to make of him a worthwhile citizen. The Negro has made great strides and the Southern white man is largely responsible for these advancements. In Mississippi, and in other Southern States, Negroes who have desired to do so have become well educated and wealthy. Millionaires are included in this group. This group has among its numbers doctors, lawyers, teachers, business men, insurance executives, merchants and plantation owners. There is no field of economic endeavor which has been barred to the Negro. It is only in the social sphere that the barrier is raised.

It is important, although painful, to quote the good Judge Brady because he represents all the platitudes that have become associated with the White Supremacists. At one time in his address, he paused to interject this adulation:

The loveliest and purest of God's creatures, the nearest thing to an angelic being that treads this terrestial ball, is a well-bred, cultured Southern white woman, or her blue-eyed, golden-haired little girl.

And on the other hand:

The Negro, in so far as sex is concerned, is not immoral, he is simply non-moral. He merely follows his natural instincts. The pregnancies and illegitimate births which have occurred in schools are not abnormal, they are merely astounding! The high percentage of venereal diseases among the Negro children is tragic. In the South, we have not and do not punish the Negro except in rare instances for desertion, illegitimacy or bigamy. To have two or more common-law wives along with a legal wife is not unusual for Negro men. The white race is now on the verge of forever abolishing incest. The Negro is still far behind. In the South, we punish the Negro for incest and there are now on my docket, as is frequently the case, indictments against Negroes who have begotten children by their daughters. We cannot count for nought the natural indolence and indifference of the Negro's nature. We cannot disregard his utter disregard for the laws relating to theft. We cannot overlook his proclivity for drunkenness and dope addiction. We cannot overlook his natural tendency to immorality and violence and subject our children to the terrible consequences resulting from such traits through integration.

Many Council members repudiated parts of Judge Brady's text, but it carried great appeal to large sections of the segregationist movement.

Another popular pamphlet, *A Christian View on Segregation*, by the Reverend Dr. G. T. Gillespie, president emeritus of Belhaven College, Mississipi, and a Presbyterian minister, purports to prove that the Bible provided ample justification for segregation. Using a combination of sophistry and agile semantics, Dr. Gillespie argues:

> While the Bible contains no clear mandate for or against segregation as between white and Negro races, it does furnish considerable data from which valid inferences may be drawn in support of the general principle of segregation as an important feature of the Divine purpose and Providence throughout the ages.

Then, using the word *separation* as a springboard, he cites Genesis to show that a "mark is placed upon Cain, and he is separated from the other branch of the human family, represented by Seth and his descendants." After the Flood, Dr. Gillespie shows, "the three sons of Noah, Shem, Ham and Japheth, became the progenitors of three distinct racial groups. The descendants of Shem migrated eastward and occupied most of Asia; the descendants of

Japheth migrated westward and ultimately occupied the continent of Europe, while the children of Ham moved generally southward toward the tropics and occupied the continent of Africa, and possibly southern Asia and the islands in the Pacific."

Sanctimoniously, Dr. Gillespie reasons:

> This brief record, the accuracy of which has not been successfully disputed by the anthropologists and ethnologists, while affirming the unity of the race, also implies that an all-wise Providence has "determined the times before appointed, and the bounds of their habitation." Which same Providence, by determining the climatic and other physical conditions under which many successive generations of the several racial groups should live, is thereby equally responsible for the distinct racial characteristics which seem to have become fixed in prehistoric times, and which are chiefly responsible for the segregation of racial groups across the centuries and in our time.

It appears, according to Dr. Gillespie, that God was always in favor of separation:

> The Confusion of Tongues, which took place at Babel, with the consequent scattering of the peoples, was an act of special Divine Providence to frustrate the mistaken efforts of godless men to assure the permanent integration of the peoples of the earth. Incidentally it indicates that the development of different languages was not merely natural or accidental, but served a Divine purpose, in becoming one of the most effective means of preserving the separate existence of the several racial groups.

Dr. Gillespie goes on at length, bending and molding each chapter and verse to his purpose. It requires pre-sympathy with the gospel according to Gillespie to agree with the twists and subjective interpretations, but that is no problem to the members of any White Supremacist group.

Having placed the Bible, Old and New Testaments, on the side of segregation, Dr. Gillespie and the Citizens' Councils, in their "educational" pamphlets, seek to show that Thomas Jefferson and Abraham Lincoln also favored separation.

The quotation from Jefferson's autobiography, volume 1, page 48, written in 1821, and confirmed on page 164 of the *Life, Writings and Opinions of Thomas Jefferson*, by B. L. Rayner (1832), is:

> Nothing is more certainly written in the book of fate than that these [Negro] people are to be free; nor is it less certain that the two races, equally free, cannot live in the same government. Nature, habit, opinion have drawn indelible lines of distinction between them. It is still in our power to direct the process of emancipation and deportation, peaceably, and in such slow degree, as that the evil will wear off insensibly, and their place be, *pari passu*, filled up by free white laborers.

In a speech made by Lincoln at Charleston, Illinois, on September 18, 1858, when he was running for the Senate against Stephen Douglas, he said:

> I will say, then, that I am not, nor ever have been, in favor of bringing about in any way the social and political equality of the white and black races; that I am not, nor ever have

been, in favor of making voters or jurors of Negroes, nor of qualifying them to hold office, nor to intermarry with white people, and I will say in addition to this that there is a physical difference between the white and black races which I believe will forever forbid the two races living together on terms of social and political equality, and inasmuch as they cannot so live, while they do remain together there must be a position of superior and inferior, and I, as much as any other man, am in favor of having the superior position assigned to the white race.

Lincoln is also quoted from an address he made to a group of free Negroes at the White House on August 14, 1862:

You and we are different races. We have between us a broader difference than exists between any other two races. Whether it is right or wrong I need not discuss, but this physical difference is a great disadvantage to us both, as I think . . . If this is admitted, it affords a reason, at least, why we should be separated.

These quotations are taken casually out of the context and philosophy of these two men whose historic attitude toward freedom and equality need not be elaborated. But the quotations give to the White Supremacist movement a sense of respectability that it sorely needs in order to offset some of the other literature it disseminates, such as *The Ugly Truth About the N.A.A.C.P.*, in which ugly untruths are repeated; an address by Senator James O. Eastland of Mississippi, *We've Reached Era of Judicial Tyranny*, in which the United States Supreme Court and the individual justices are condemned; *Mixed Schools and Mixed*

Blood, in which all the worn-out clichés of racism are repeated, and *A Jewish View on Segregation,* in which an anonymous Southern Jew "proves" that segregation is the best thing for the South and the North as well. As in the case of other extremist groups, the private axe-grinders made their pitch and in some areas there was distribution of standard anti-Catholic literature; the *Williams Intelligence Summary,* an anti-Semitic tract, and the usual number of anti-labor and anti-United Nations pamphlets.

The Councils gained their initial support and their strongest leadership from the black-belt sections, which have a plantation economy and heritage and where Negroes generally outnumber the whites. This pattern was easily seen in Mississippi, South Carolina and Alabama. Economic reprisals against Negroes who dared speak up, and threats of night riders, were made by groups headed by Asa (Ace) Carter, in Northern Alabama, and John Kasper, executive secretary of the Seaboard White Citizens' Council.

Carter was expelled from his state association because of his extremist approach and Kasper went to jail for inciting violence. But both men continued to operate in the backwoods areas, spellbinding crowds of rednecks, white trash, sharecroppers, town loafers and the horde of social malcontents who have elevated their own meager egos by hatred of the Negro.

These two and others like them found eager audiences among the hoodlum elements in Arkansas, Alabama, Georgia, Louisiana, Mississippi, North and South Carolina, Tennessee and Texas. Kasper's venom came out in a pamphlet called *Virginians on Guard,* in which he urged: "Hang the nine Supreme Court swine; destroy all Reds, Rooseveltian dupes, and death to usurers." He told all Southerners to refuse to obey Federal Government orders on segregation and demanded that local officials arrest any Federal judge or FBI agent who interfered.

The moderates in the Councils, those who sought merely to maintain status-quo segregation, deplored such activities. Charges of witch-hunting were made against Council groups that attempted to create thought control in all areas, especially in schools, libraries and churches. All the old familiar bedfellows of extremism joined in fighting labor, social legislation and any kind of progress under the coverall of segregation.

Oliver Emmerich, the conservative editor of the *State Times* of Jackson, Mississippi, spoke out bravely when he wrote:

> There is a growing belief that witch-hunting and book-burning should be tolerated. The idea advanced is that the end justifies the means. But witch-hunting . . . is just as wicked in Mississippi as in Russia. And book-burning is as wrong when practiced in our state as when it was practiced by Hitler's Germans. The tragic truth about this secret-police procedure is that it is advanced by well-meaning citizens. It is being done in the name of patriotism.

An editor in rural Mississippi also battled against thought control. L. H. Howell, editor of *The Panolian*, a weekly at Batesville, in the north central part of the state, charged that

> the State Department of Education was forced to ban the use of an educational film—not because the film was offen-

sive, but because its producers were not on a list of organizations approved by the Citizens' Council. Most people know that the Methodist Church and the United States Air Force have been listed as enemies of the Citizens' Council, along with other denominations and agencies. One questions whether the reading of the Bible soon is to be restricted in the same manner that Nazi Germany sought to rid the Reich of all "subversive influence," literary and otherwise.

But this editorial criticism and the restraints attempted by the moderates within the Citizens' Councils did not deter or even slow the movement, which was fiercely dedicated to "protect itself from the Negro's new-found ambitions." As the government moved to integrate schools, reprisals, economic and physical began to take place. A list of the beatings, threats and riots will some day show how they strengthened the Negro purpose and forwarded the drive to integration. But the road was hard and steep and the top has not yet been reached.

Already fading into bitter history are the shameful incidents at Little Rock; Montgomery; Clinton, Tennessee; Sturgis, Kentucky; Beaumont, Texas; Orangeburg, South Carolina, and New Orleans.

In each instance it was the Citizens' Council followers trying to stop the integration of a school. There were heroes and villains, but as time went on these schools were integrated, some in a token fashion and some completely.

While the nation, and the free world, were looking on in dismay at this display of atavism, there were bright spots that showed integration was possible with peace and dignity. In Louisville, Kentucky, the Board of Education faced the same racist pressures as any other Southern board. But its members moved swiftly and firmly. All schools were re-districted. Parents were permitted to request transfers for their children. Some Negroes did not want to risk the first resentment of integration and asked to remain in Negro schools. Some whites could not bear the thought of their children attending mixed schools. These were accommodated wherever possible. Louisville was frankly getting the support of the moderates, who were being conditioned by a plan of psychologically spaced announcements. The news-papers, *The Courier-Journal* and *The Times*, showed cour-age by supporting the plans and urging the parents to show decency and cooperation. Integration was achieved without furore or even fanfare. As one white parent said: "This is an American city and we're doing this in the Amer-ican way." And one minister remarked from the pulpit: "It's good to hear the phrase, *American way*, used in its proper sense."

Van Buren, Arkansas, has a population of 6,400, com-pared with the 400,000 in Louisville. The town never had a Negro high school, and its Negro elementary school looked like part of the set from *Tobacco Road*. When the Supreme Court decision became known, Sam Cox, Jr., a truck driver, decided the town ought to have a Citizens' Council. The Reverend Grady Williams ordained himself to be treasurer. A few speeches were made. No one in Van Buren lis-tened. There were only ten young Negroes eligible for high school. Under the separate but equal ruling, a special school would have to be built for them. So the schools were inte-grated. But some of the students, about 70 of them, in-vaded the school and chased the Negro children out.

"These were the dregs who can't make it from one grade

to another," said Calvin Patterson, the high school principal. The townspeople were shocked at the action. But
school officials moved swiftly. They expelled the 70 unruly
ones, and agreed to readmit them only on the understanding that a repetition of their hooliganism would mean permanent dismissal. The Negro children went back. Van Buren was quiet. Integration was complete.

As integration became more widespread and the Negroes
gained knowledge and courage, the reprisals became more
intense. In Montgomery, Alabama, the Reverend Martin
Luther King led a boycott of the segregated buses which
was won after a long and bitter struggle. There were incidents at lunch counters, bus depots and trains. The Negroes continued to win their battles, aided by the Federal
courts. In Birmingham, Alabama, city officials retaliated
against a Negro boycott of department stores that accepted
their trade but refused to hire them or serve them at lunch
counters, by cutting off funds for government surplus foods
for the needy, most of whom were Negroes. The Citizens'
Councils looked upon this as a test and a possible blueprint
for similar actions elsewhere. But there was no doubt that
in the long run the Negroes, firmly dedicated to their own
program of lawful defiance of all the old and tired prejudices, would win, quietly and decisively.

One of the great disappointments in the program of the
White Supremacists has been their failure to incite the Negroes to violence. Wherever the Negroes have defied the
rules and traditions of the South they have done so with
peace and dignity. Every time a White Supremacist shouts,
rants, raves and threatens, the Negroes follow the admonition of their leaders: "Love, Law and Liberation." One Ne-

gro minister said from the pulpit that, "if Jesus Christ came to South Carolina and spoke for integration, he would be stoned from the state."

Another area where the White Citizens' Council is finding an embarrassing boomerang is in the qualification of voters. In order to make voting difficult, if not impossible, for Negroes, one Citizens' Council in Minden, Louisiana, ordered the strict enforcement of voter qualification rules. Among those who failed the test were 24 white applicants. This incident has been repeated countless times in areas throughout the South and the White Supremacists have decided on a re-examination of this strategy.

In the years since "Black Monday" there has been a steady growth in membership of the Citizens' Councils and their various affiliates. There has been no slackening in their activities and their finances have grown stronger. Merchants and businessmen are pressured to contribute to the cost of the vast literature that is filling the United States mails. Generally dues are about $10 a year, with varying amounts for initiation fees. Contributions come in from "interests" in large amounts, and are administered by the local groups as they see fit. Although the Association of Citizens' Councils is presumed to be the central authority, there is no fixed discipline in the movement, since all members are committed to the single aim of fighting integration.

The tragic conflict between Southern tradition and religious obedience captured the attention of the entire country when Roman Catholic Archbishop Joseph Francis Rummel of New Orleans ordered the integration of all parochial schools in his diocese. There was wrath, chagrin and strong protest from most of his parishioners, who felt that Catholic schools did not come under the Supreme Court ruling. But Archbishop Rummel stated clearly that the time had come for integration, and, when he threatened to excommunicate those who disobeyed, almost all his people complied.

Only three defied the Archbishop's ruling.

The first was "Judge" Leander H. Perez, the aging, oil-rich, cigar-smoking political dictator of Louisiana's Plaquemines Parish (county), a stronghold of racism and segregation. He charged that the Archbishop had stepped beyond his powers and that, anyway, desegregation was nothing more than a Communist-Zionist conspiracy. Unrepentant, he told a White Citizens' rally to deprive the church of financial support. "Cut off their water," he shouted, "and see how soon they'll come around to our way of seeing this integration matter."

The second was Jackson G. Ricau, executive secretary of the South Louisiana Citizens' Council, who called Rummel's action an "incredible injustice." He, too, remained unrepentant and wrote to the Archbishop: "Of course I will continue to fight integration. I am fighting for the survival of the white race under the banner of the Constitution, to defend that great document, and to oppose Communist operations in the integration movement. Such a battle should merit warm ecclesiastical approval."

The third and most dramatic was Mrs. B. J. Gaillot, author of a pamphlet, *God Gave the Law of Segregation to Moses on Mount Sinai*. To the astonishment of her fellow-Catholics, she indicated she knew more about her religion than the Archbishop. "God demands the segregation of the races," she said, "and curses all integrators no matter who they are." In support of her private dogma she cited Old Testament sources, including Numbers: 36-9-10: "And that the tribes be not mingled with one another but remain so as they are separated by the Lord." As the leader of a women's segregationist group called Save Our Nation, Inc., she declared desperately that "it can't be any other way . . . it just can't."

The day after her excommunication, Mrs. Gaillot confronted her spiritual leader in person. Rummel was standing on the lawn in front of his residence, greeting 15 women on an annual pilgrimage to the shrine of Our Lady of Fatima, when Mrs. Gaillot appeared. She walked swiftly past the 20 pickets who were peacefully protesting the desegregation order, marched on to the lawn and threw herself on her knees in front of the Archbishop.

"Forgive me for coming here while you are engaged in prayers," she said shrilly. The astonished Archbishop never lost his composure. He stared over her head as she spoke, grimly refusing to acknowledge her presence.

"I ask your blessing, Your Excellency," she pleaded, "but I want to tell you that I am not apologizing for anything that I have done in the past. I beg God's mercy that you know in your heart that you had nothing to do with my excommunication."

Several women from the pilgrimage urged Rummel not to answer her. Two approached her and she shouted: "Don't put your hands on me . . . don't put your hands on me." Then the women began chanting "Hail, Mary, full of grace. . . ." Mrs. Gaillott continued to chatter, almost incoherently. She did not resist when some of the women took her arms and led her away as the Archbishop turned his back on her and walked slowly and silently back to his residence. The next day her husband asked the Archbishop to excommunicate him, too.

The imposition of the severe penalty of excommunication—exclusion from Mass, the Sacraments and Catholic burial—were not surprising to those who understood the attitude of the Archbishop. He had begun preaching racial justice as far back as 1948, and in 1956 he declared segregation to be morally wrong. He moved slowly to avoid wild disruption of his school system and was encouraged by successful integration in other Southern states such as Texas and Florida.

There was a great deal of grumbling among the faithful when the order was issued, but one observer declared that the "majority will go along; no one is kicking over the traces. Catholics still regard the Archbishop as top man. He's been here so long—he's the only Archbishop New Orleans Catholics have ever known."

Rummel's move also encouraged other Catholic prelates in the South. Bishop Robert E. Tracy of Baton Rouge strongly supported Rummel's stand and indicated that the time was near for all Catholics in the South to see the light.

The nagging frustration engendered by the steady gains of integration has stimulated attempts to embarrass great Negro centers such as New York, Chicago, Los Angeles and Detroit. The Citizens' Council of Greater New Orleans began to purchase one-way tickets for poor Negro families and succeeded in sending a few to New York, Chicago and Hyannis Port, Mass., President Kennedy's summer home.

Much was made of the gratitude of the Negroes for being given a chance to go North. New York received them hospitably, managed to find work for them and soundly condemned the New Orleans group for victimizing these innocent people.

George L. Singelmann, a member of the Council's board of directors, who took charge of the "exodus," promised that plans were being made to send a "freedom bus" north each week. Singelmann insisted that the action was sincere. "The North can now show how hospitable it is—it can put up or shut up. We will pay one-way fares for any Negro who wants to leave here and go north. There's plenty of white money to pay for this."

The action was condemned as a propaganda stunt by Loretha Castle, chairman of the New Orleans Congress of Racial Equality. "It is unrealistic," she said, "and the Negroes who do consent to be used in this manner are the unemployed, the uneducated who feel that they are being presented with a rare gift."

New York, especially, is regarded as a prime villain in the integration movement and the fountainhead of all the pro-Negro propaganda. White Supremacists never fail to include that city in their vituperation and, when an opportunity presents itself to embarrass New York, the racists are delighted. Indeed, it has been suspected that the Citizens' Councils plan to place New York in an awkward position whenever possible. Their speakers always refer to the Harlem ghetto, its muggings and rapings and saloon fights.

It is true that New York is discussed by Negroes in the deep South in awesome tones as a haven and a heaven where the Negro has equality; where he can dine in any restaurant if he has the price; go to any theater and sit in the orchestra; sit in the grandstand at baseball and football games and generally take in all the pleasures of the city on a brotherly basis with the white man. There are also the stories of New York's fabulous relief agencies, where poor and indigent Negroes are provided for and treated with decency and dignity. It was on the strength of this knowledge that some White Supremacist with a cruel sense of humor, at best, or a vicious intent, hoped to create an incident.

One day, Negroes in the poor sections of Savannah, Georgia, and Pachuta, Mississippi, found in their grocery stores and barber shops neatly printed handbills that said:

INFORMATION

FOR THOSE WHO WISH TO GO TO NEW YORK

Welfare Center
157 East 67th Street
Phone Lehigh 5-4200
New York, N. Y.

Upon arriving in New York you should apply at the above address immediately for benefits which are available to all new arrivals to the area. A nice apartment with private bathroom, lights, gas, continuous hot and cold water, food, clothing, hospital care, doctors' care, medicine, child care services of a house keeper and home nursing service plus a cash living allowance—which depends on the size of the family.

There are no limitations on the amount of cash contributed by the welfare.

North of New York labor workers receive from 70 to 80 dollars weekly.

There is no time limitation on welfare rolls and one need not be a legal resident to receive the above services—which are available upon applying at the office.

Fine schools and churches are available in all areas of the state without restriction or discrimination because of race, creed or national origin.

W. W. Law, president of the Georgia N.A.A.C.P., believed that the handbills were part of a White Citizens' Council campaign against Negroes intended to "injure race relations" and embarrass the officials in the North. W. E. Cowart, president of the Chatham Citizens' Council, said this was a trick by extremists, implying that the extremists were Negroes. "Those who might react to this," he said, "are innocents who might borrow money and put themselves in debt to go to a place like New York only to find the dream exploded."

James R. Dumpson, New York's Welfare Commissioner, said his department had nothing to do with the circulation of the handbills. Nor does it have an office at 157 East 67th Street. Peter Kasius, the deputy commissioner, said the handbills must have been distributed by persons "anxious to stir up racial tensions with promises that were cruel, vicious and misleading." All New York agencies reported that there had been no influx of Negroes from the two towns where the handbills were distributed.

The Negro cause has its newer martyrs: On May 9, 1955, the Reverend G. W. Lee of Belzoni, Mississippi, was fatally shot after he urged Negro voters to register at election time. In the same town, Gus Courts became active in interracial work and was shot. There were others, unknown and unrecorded, who suffered injury and deprivation for standing up against segregation. The most celebrated case was that of Autherine Lucy, who was driven from the campus of the University of Alabama by rioters led by Citizens' Council students. These students shocked the Southern community by issuing a leaflet that said:

> When in the course of human events it becomes necessary to abolish the Negro race, proper methods should be used. Among them are guns, bows and arrows, slingshots and knives. We hold these truths to be self-evident: that all whites are created with certain rights; among these are life, liberty and the pursuit of dead niggers.

There was one unpleasant truth that the Citizens' Councils tried to ignore. Bigotry and hatred were dangerous traditions that tortured the parents and incited their children. One Negro clergyman in a tiny village in the wasteland of deepest Alabama said: "In the long run we will win because nothing, nobody, can live on hate alone."

13. Only black is right

Malcolm Little, a lean, ascetic-looking man in his thirties with searching eyes, faced his eager and attentive audience at the Boston University School of Theology. He was there for the precise purpose of verifying or destroying a set of myths and conceptions about America's newest and most controversial racist group, the Black Muslims. He said that his new name was Malcolm X; that he was a minister of Temple of Islam Number Seven in New York's Harlem, and that he and almost 200,000 other members of the Black Race were fanatical followers of "the most fearless Black Man in America—Elijah Muhammad."

His six-foot frame, leaning forward intently, his thick horn-rimmed spectacles and his clear, concise language gave his audience the impression he sought to convey—that of a scholarly young man imparting important information. Malcolm X was speaking with his customary sincerity that seemed to mesmerize his audience to heed every precious word he was uttering.

"All who follow Elijah Muhammad have given their slave names back to the white man," he said. "We don't call ourselves Negroes any longer. We are Black Muslims. We have given back to the white man, along with our chains, his whisky, his dope, his politics, his religion and all his other vices. We reject his blue-eyed God. Islam is the natural religion of black mankind. We are never aggressors. We will not attack anyone. We strive for peaceful relationships with everyone. But we do teach our people that, if anyone attacks you, lay down your life. Every Muslim is taught never to start a fight. Respect another man's rights whether he is white, black, brown or yellow. Respect him as a man. But if any man molests you, may Allah bless you."

Quoting profusely from the writings and addresses of Muhammad, Minister Malcolm X pointed out that, in "begging for integration during all those long years, the Negro barely attracted the white man's attention. But we've shaken up the white man by asking for separation. To beg the white man to let you eat in his restaurant is just feeding his ego. What we feel is that after more than 300 years of labor the black man is worth more than a cup of coffee in a white restaurant or a house in a cracker neighborhood. We Muslims mean to collect the black man's long overdue back wages."

Malcolm X specified that the Black Muslims wanted a land grant somewhere along the eastern seaboard from the Federal government, as well as money to help build a separate state. He estimated that this land would occupy as much as one-fifth of the nation's territory. He admitted that this scheme was grandiose, ambitious and not likely to come to fruition in the near future, but he pointed out to his startled audience that those "Black Pharisees, middle-class black men satisfied with conditions as they are, who denounce the Black Muslims, find secret joy and pride in these demands." Then, calmly, he revealed that he was an ex-convict. "A lot of our people are ex-dope addicts, ex-bums, ex-Negroes and ex-Christians. And a lot have been upper-class citizens all their lives, respectable, well-to-do and thoroughly fed up with being second-class citizens in a white man's society."

(Police records show that Muhammad, under the name of Poole, served three years for draft-dodging in World War II, and that Malcolm X, under the name of Little, served time for procuring and was arrested on charges of larceny in two states.)

The remarks by Malcolm X that "shook up" the Boston audience had already disturbed the stable Negro community in the United States. In their long and tortured ascent from slavery toward equality, American Negroes had faced many enemies whose colors were easy to recognize. They knew the unreconstructed whites in the South as well as in the North who consciously practiced patronizing benevolence to prove that the Negro could be happy "in his proper place," but who also made it clear that the kindly hand could be clenched into an iron first if the Negro broke the white man's rules. Organizations such as the National Association for the Advancement of Colored People and the Urban League had fought for the betterment of the Negro within the framework provided by American tradition and law, and had avoided extreme policies or actions. They were able to point to progressively increasing successes and looked with dismay at the Muslim policy of separation, which they regarded as unrealistic as well as unwelcome. Yet Roy Wilkins, executive secretary of the N.A.A.C.P., could not resist using the Black Muslims to make a traditional point.

"The surprise [of the whites] that American Negroes identify with the Africans illustrates how far our white public is from realizing the repression and the treatment of the Negro in this country," he said. "The solution, of course, is the complete acceptance and partnership of the Negro in American life so that he is in truth a citizen equal with other citizens instead of theoretically equal."

A similar position was taken by Edward S. Lewis, executive director of the Urban League of Greater New York, who declared that "we have to eliminate the inequities in our society in three pivotal fields—education, employment and housing." Only this would take away the ammunition from the extremist groups.

Another highly influential Negro leader, the Rev. Martin Luther King, while condemning the Black Muslims, showed that the extremist philosophy had the virtue of dramatizing the plight of the Negro. "The doctrine of black supremacy," he said, "is as dangerous as the doctrine of white supremacy, but, while we must condemn their philosophy, we must also understand the conditions which breed this type of philosophy. The government must remove these conditions or such groups as this will continue to emerge."

In his excellent study on the American Negro in general and the Black Muslims in particular, C. Eric Lincoln, professor of social philosophy at Clark College in Atlanta and an ordained Methodist Minister, suggests that the "tradition of disprivilege and the continuing formidable opposition to first-class citizenship are the discouraging elements that contribute most to the Muslim mood."

Historians and sociologists agree that "the mood" had its genesis in the days of slavery and shortly thereafter, but that it was buried deeply under layers of ignorance and illiteracy. Early attempts to unite the Negroes in some form of political movement failed, but the religious appeal was strong, and in 1913 a Negro from North Carolina named Timothy Drew established a Moorish Science Temple in Newark, New Jersey, and proceeded to encourage a new identity for his followers. He changed his own name to Noble Drew Ali and decreed that all American Negroes were to be known as "Asiatics," "Moors," or "Moorish Americans." Prof. Lincoln writes that Drew documented this ethnic transformation by issuing Nationality Identification Cards. "Each card," Lincoln recalls, "bore the Islamic symbol [the star and crescent], an image of clasped hands, and a numeral 7 in a circle. It announced that the bearer honored all the Divine Prophets, Jesus, Mohammed, Buddha, and Confucius, and pronounced upon him the blessings of the God of our fathers, Allah. It identified him as a Moslem under the Divine Laws of the Holy Koran of Mecca, Love, Truth, Peace, Freedom, and Justice, and concluded with the assurance: 'I am a citizen of the United States.' Each card was validated by the subscription: *Noble Drew Ali, the Prophet*."

Temples were established in New York, Chicago, Detroit, Philadelphia, Pittsburgh and smaller cities throughout the South. It was estimated that membership reached 30,000. The members caused quite a stir in the "white" cities with their picturesque fezzes and boisterous behav-

ior in their new-found "freedom." As the movement bur-
geoned, it expanded beyond the capacity of Drew to ad-
minister it. Exploiters foisted magical potions, charms and
relics upon the gullible followers, growing rich on the proceeds. When it was evident that Drew was an obstacle to
this exploitation, he was slain. The circumstances were
never fully told, but it was believed he was fatally beaten
by his own rivals.

The heritage that Drew left for the Black Muslims was
the creed that "Christianity is for the European (pale
face); Moslemism is for the Asiatic (olive-skinned). Religious faith shall not cross racial lines, and, when each
group has its own peculiar religion, there will be peace on
earth."

After Drew's death (exact date unknown but believed to
be some time in the 1920's) his followers split into many
groups. Even today there are some Moorish temples left in
Negro communities of the larger cities, and it is significant
that many Moors were among the earliest converts to the
Black Muslim Movement. They swiftly recognized Elijah
Muhammad as a strong, uncompromising leader who would
help preserve their Asiatic religion without asking them to
love their "pale-faced brethren."

The Black Muslim Movement learned a great deal from
Noble Drew Ali, but it owes even a greater debt to Marcus
Garvey, who came upon the American scene shortly after
World War I. It was a time when American Negroes felt
they had earned some rewards for their monumental labors
in fields and factories at home and on battlefields in Europe
to help win the war. Instead, they returned to an intensi-
fied bigotry that manifested itself in tragic repressions and

violence. In the first 14 months after the war, 70 Negroes were lynched, including a number still in their Army khakis. White men burned 14 Negroes in public, 11 while still alive. There were at least 25 race riots of record. A riot in Washington took three days to put down. Chicago went through 13 days of mob rule during which 38 were killed and more than 500 were injured. Ghetto lines were clearly drawn and policed, creating virtual residential prison areas for Negroes in the larger cities. Authorities pointed out, with some truth, that these measures were designed to keep the hoodlum elements, black and white, from getting at each other. But this applied only to overt violence. Riding high in their nightshirts were the members of the Ku Klux Klan, which had been revived and was making significant progress in the so-called enlightened New England states and New York as well as in Illinois, Indiana and Michigan.

Whatever smoldering race conflicts were being brought to the surface at the time, they were not considered the prime cause for the outbreaks. The true villain was economics. The Negro veterans who had served in Europe had been exposed to freedom and equality they had never experienced before. They came back disillusioned with the portion of democracy their own country was prepared to give them. The post-war depression brought about increasingly fierce competition for jobs and housing between white and black in the marginal areas. Negroes were forced into a race consciousness that was developing into race chauvinism. The traditional passive resistance in thought and action was rapidly giving way to resistance in deeds. Even some of the more sympathetic whites were complaining of the "new arrogance" of the post-war Negro.

Garvey, a native of Jamaica in the British West Indies, went to New York in 1916, started with street-corner speeches and, having failed to attract attention, toured 38 states to study conditions of Negro life. He concluded a year later that the so-called Negro leaders were mere opportunists who had no program and were living off the poor people who were blundering in the dark. He had already formed the Universal Negro Improvement Association under the compelling motto of "One God. One Aim. One Destiny." He urged all people of Negro or African parentage to help him to "establish a Universal Confraternity among the race; to promote the spirit of race pride and love; to reclaim the fallen of the race; to strengthen the self-determination of independent African states; to establish universities, colleges and secondary schools for the further education and culture of the boys and girls of the race, and to conduct a world-wide commercial and industrial intercourse."

The aggressive, flamboyant Garvey was held at first in scorn and then in fear by the Negro leaders of the day whom he had criticized for depending so heavily upon white philanthrophy. He was described by one as a "Jamaican of unmixed stock, fat and sleek, with protruding jaws, and heavy jowls, small, bright, pig-like eyes and rather bulldog-like face. Boastful, egotistical, tyrannical, intolerant, cunning, shifty, smooth and suave, avaricious, gifted at self-advertisement, without shame in self-laudation, without regard for veracity, a lover of pomp and tawdry finery and garish display."

In spite of the attitude of the established leaders, or possibly because of it, since many militant Negroes were seeking positive action rather than vague promises, Garvey's organization grew steadily until by the summer of 1919 he was able to claim a membership of 2,000,000 in 30 branches. He published a newspaper, *The Negro World*, which was printed in English, French, and Spanish and claimed that its 200,000 circulation was reaching the mass of Negroes throughout the world. It was in this publication that Garvey gave the Negro pride and stature, laying the groundwork for the later policies of the Black Muslims. The paper ran articles stressing the Negro's contribution to history. It covered areas from heroic slave rebellions in America to the romances of the great Hottentot and Zulu wars, and the important histories of the Moorish and Ethiopian empires.

For the first time a mass circulation publication was informing the ordinary Negroes of their greatness and their potential greatness. "Up, you mighty race," Garvey exhorted, "you can accomplish what you will."

The Negroes responded with an awesome enthusiasm never witnessed before. They put millions of dollars into Garvey's Black Star Steamship Line, intended to "transport America's black millions back to their African home." They supported cooperative grocery stores, laundries, restaurants and hotels. They showed their pride in joining the Universal Black Cross Nurses, the Universal Motor Corps, the Black Eagle Flying Corps and the Universal African Legion.

Without using the words *black supremacy* or *separation*, Garvey gave the Negroes of his time a powerful awareness that in united and intelligent action they could move forward to a goal—a goal he left intentionally vague.

Because they believed that Garvey intended to lead all American Negroes to a promised land in Africa, the Ku Klux Klan and the white racists gave him their open support. Later Garvey modified his position by declaring that "we do not want all the Negroes to settle in Africa. Some are no good here and naturally will be no good there." He did put forth a plan to build a state somewhere in Africa to which "the best Negroes from all over the world" would bring their technical and professional skills. With a population of this sort, he dreamed, the new state (a sort of Black Zionism) would achieve power and prestige and stand as a symbol of what Negroes could do if given the opportunity. Elijah Muhammad borrowed freely from this philosophy that the Negro will have peace and dignity only when he is separated from the white society.

When Garvey said Africa, he meant all Africa. He told a white audience: "We say to the white man who now dominates Africa that it is to his interest to clear out of Africa now, because we are coming 400,000,000 strong. We shall not ask England or France or Belgium or Italy: 'Why are you here?' We shall command them: 'Get out of here.' " Politically these remarks were to bring his downfall later, but meanwhile Garvey was busy extending his social and religious program. Like many other Negroes brought up in a Christian tradition, Garvey resented seeing Jesus always depicted as a pure Caucasian with a white God and an all-white heavenly host. He decided the Negro God must be black.

He found a ready ally in the Rev. Alexander McGuire, a former Episcopalian priest who had battled vainly for independent status for the Negro congregations within the church and finally had organized the Independent Episcopalian Church. He took his following into the Garvey movement, changing the name to the African Orthodox Church, and then succeeded in gaining compelling ecclesiastical stature by being ordained a bishop by Archbishop Vilatte of the Syrian Orthodox Church. This brought his new African Orthodox Church into direct apostolic succession within one of the ancient bodies of organized Christendom.

Bishop McGuire told his flock: "Forget the white gods. Erase the white gods from your hearts. Be true to the principles of Christianity without the shameful hypocrisy of the white churches." Within a few years, pictures of a black Christ and a black Madonna and Child were prominent in the homes of the faithful.

By 1924 the Garvey movement was at the crest of its power and popularity, but already the forces of destruction were gaining on it. Various governmental agencies were harassing the organization with investigations; the United States was openly hostile to Garvey's international ambitions. The Department of Justice cited his newspaper for radicalism and sedition. Finally Great Britain and France, increasingly alarmed over his pledge to take over Africa with Liberia as a beachhead, brought enough pressure on that republic to force its president, Charles D. B. King, into drastic action. He informed the United States that he was "irrevocably opposed both in principle and in fact to the incendiary policy of the Universal Negro Improvement Association headed by Marcus Garvey." The territory set aside for Garvey was leased to the Firestone Rubber Corporation, and a newly-arrived Garvey mission was arrested and immediately deported.

But Garvey was encountering resistance from a more important quarter. In spite of repressions, the early Twenties had seen the emergence of a powerful Negro middle class that was beginning to make itself felt in local city elections in the North. This group and the increasing number of Negro intellectuals began to belabor Garvey's movement as "bombastic and impractical." Their attacks proved effective because, as the bourgeoisie grew in number and influence, more Negroes drifted away from Garvey into the more stable organizations that sought to benefit the race not by unattainable promises but by practical programs. In 1922, at the insistence of the Negro press, Garvey had been indicted on charges of using the mails to defraud in the promotion of shares in his steamship venture. In 1925 he was convicted and sentenced to five years. In 1927 President Coolidge commuted his sentence and he was deported because he had never become an American citizen. He sought to keep the movement going, but in the absence of his acknowledged "magic" it faded. He died obscurely in London in 1940. The author, interviewing scores of intelligent Negroes under the age of 35, learned that the name of Marcus Garvey recalled nothing to them. To a few he was a vague name mentioned occasionally by their parents. The same applied to Noble Drew Ali.

The memory of these two men was still fresh, however, in the Negro communities in 1930 when a mysterious but friendly peddler appeared in Detroit's depression-ridden

Negro section. He called himself Wallace Fard, Farrad Mohammad or F. Mohammad Ali—the word *mister* always preceding the name. He sold oriental artifacts and colorful silks from door to door and described his wares as being the kind that Negro people wore in Africa. He lingered in the homes, telling enchanting stories about Negroes in their homeland, and soon his customers, eager to hear more, gathered with him in small meetings. He was believed to be an Arab, and after a short time he was referred to as the Prophet.

As the meetings attracted more of the depressed and desperate Negroes seeking some solace from their unemployment and the harassment by police and welfare workers, Fard rented a hall, called it the Temple of Islam, and did not object when some of his faithful referred to themselves as Black Moslems or Muslims. Within a short time the informal gatherings were replaced by an efficient organization and a tight discipline. Fard wrote a number of pamphlets recounting the Black Man's Destiny under Allah; he set up the fixed Moslem or Muslim ritual and developed well-trained deputies. He founded a University of Islam, a combined elementary and secondary school, and created a Muslim Girls' Training Class that instructed the young women in home economics and how to be a proper wife and mother. Then, for "internal and external discipline," he set up the Fruit of Islam—a fully constituted military organization where the use of firearms was taught. To this day it is the official policing agency of the Black Muslims.

Fard, who had revealed himself to his followers as "Allah on Earth," achieved a wraithlike, mystic quality that added power to his preachments. He proceeded to withdraw from direct executive functions, appointing Ministers of Islam to conduct the affairs of the organization and report to him in private communion. Among the first to join this select *échelon* was a Negro from Georgia, Elijah Poole, who was given the name of Elijah Muhammad. He was fierce in his devotion to Fard and the cause, and, although opposed by the few moderates in power, he became the leader's most trusted captain. In the end, when a chief Minister had to be chosen, Fard designated Muhammad.

Schisms began to show within two years, especially after Fard insisted upon teaching and repeating that his faithful were not Americans and therefore owed no allegiance to the American flag. He told them it "was stupid to pledge allegiance to a flag that offered no protection against the depravities of the white devils who by their *tricknology* keep our peoples illiterate to use as tools and slaves." One group broke off and swore complete loyalty to the American Constitution. The Communist Party tried infiltration and failed. The Japanese tried to use the Muslims as a foundation for a "fifth column" and failed, even though a few members did swear allegiance to the Mikado (whoever he might be). The Ethiopians sought to use the Black Muslims in a variety of financial deals, and failed. Even union-breaking organizations sought to use the Muslim members in their fight against the CIO, and failed.

By this time, Elijah Muhammad was publicly deifying Fard, thus increasing his own importance. Suddenly, in June, 1934, Fard vanished. His disappearance was as mysterious as his arrival. There were reports that he had been seen aboard a ship bound for Europe; that he had met with foul play at the hands of some dissidents or even the Detroit police, or that some "white groups had finally tired of his anti-Christian diatribes and chased him away." None of this was substantiated and his disappearance remains unsolved.

The true leader gone, fragmentation took place in the Black Muslim organization. The moderates forced Muhammad to leave Temple Number One in Detroit and move to Temple Number Two in Chicago, where he attracted active and aggressive followers under a militant uncompromising program. Fard was equated with Allah; therefore Muhammad, who had served him, became the Prophet and the Messenger of Allah. Having gathered about him only the intense, the fanatic and the true believers, Muhammad moved in the direction of black supremacy with a clear and outspoken policy. In one of his early speeches, to be repeated countless times in the years to come, Muhammad declared that "every white man knows his time is up. I am here to teach you how to be free. Yes, free from the white man's yoke. We want unity of all darker peoples on earth. Then we will be masters of the United States, and we are going to treat the white man the way he should be treated." He denounced the "white devils, the satisfied black men, the poison Bible, Christianity's slavemaster doctrine and white for white justice."

Muhammad made no secret of the fact that the Black Muslims were seeking to satisfy the rankling frustrations of city Negroes, but he had no intention of being the leader of a shapeless mob. He introduced a fixed discipline and warned his followers that this was not a "Sunday religion." He commanded the men to hold on to their jobs, live respectably, provide for their families and be proud of their race. All members were forbidden to smoke, gamble, drink liquor, overeat, indulge in frivolities or buy on credit. Muslims were told to contribute up to one-third of their earnings to the movement. "The money saved on liquor and fripperies," Muhammad said, "would be enough to take care of that expenditure."

The earliest followers of Muhammad were Negroes from the rural South who had migrated north during the depression. They were joined by the most disprivileged members of the Negro communities in the North. The predominantly male membership was between 17 and 35 years of age. Women were given dignity and honor, were required to perform duties within a defined area and generally shared in the business of the organization—but with the clearly understood policy that the males were the rulers and held the prime responsibility in all matters, private and public.

The Muslims continue to encourage this kind of membership. Recruiting is mostly from low-income groups at the lowest rung of the educational level. Factory workers, domestics, laborers and the unemployed as well as the unemployables are encouraged to join. In recent years, because of the public outcry from established Negro organizations, rebels among the Negro intellectuals have joined in increasing numbers. As one young college graduate with a promising job in the Federal Government explained: "The Black Muslims are active, vibrant and alive. Perhaps they do have an impossible dream. But there are many among us who need an impossible dream because striving for it may lead us closer to the ultimate goal than all the practical ideas."

Prof. Lincoln points out that the "fundamental attraction of the Black Muslim Movement is its passion for group solidarity, its exaggerated sense of consciousness-of-kind. What matters above all is that men acknowledge themselves as black or white, and that all black men work together to accomplish their group aims." One Muslim minister said fiercely that he wanted to "get the white man's foot off my neck, his hand out of my pocket and his carcass off my back; to sleep in my own bed without fear and to look straight into his cold blue eyes and call him a liar every time he parts his lips." The ultimate appeal of the Movement, therefore, is the chance to become identified with a power strong enough to overcome the domination of the white man—and perhaps even to subordinate him in turn.

American Negroes have always been a religious people, generally Protestant, and the Muslims' strong anti-Christian tone has caused considerable concern. Yet it has been common knowledge that an increasing number of Negroes of all classes are disillusioned by the continuance of racial segregation in many churches. The mildest charge against these churches is apathy. The Muslims have made capital of this historic rejection.

By the way of paradox, the Black Muslims have evoked the wrath of America's 100,000 true Moslems, who denounce the bastardization of the ancient faith, especially in the matter of black supremacy. The Moslems point to their traditional position against racial discrimination of

any kind, citing chapter 49, verse, 13, from the Koran:
All mankind we created
You are from a single pair
Of a male and a female
And made you into
Nations and tribes
Ye may know each other
Not that ye may despise
Each other.

American Moslems do not wish to be identified in any manner with the Black Muslims. Since it is clearly not a matter of race, the rejection is based on Elijah Muhammad's unhistoric teachings, his extremist views on race and his uncompromising militancy. One Moslem leader, Jamil Diab of Chicago, denounced the Black Muslims as "a cult totally lacking in the requisites which constitute any Moslem group. They have penetrated into the Afro-American society . . . where they propagate their views in the name of Islam. They start controversies everywhere and carry on propaganda in an aggressive manner. Because of them an insidious stigma has become attached to all Islamic societies in America."

Muhammad, however, contends that Diab and the other Moslems at first sought to form the Black Muslims into an orthodox Moslem organization, but, since none of the followers of Muhammad approved of the idea, the Moslems withdrew. This increased the power of Muhammad, who, with his ministers, enjoys a kind of papal absolutism in the development of his own movement. It has also made it possible for Muhammad and Malcolm X to develop the good will and respect of members of Afro-

Asian Islam, who frequently visit the temples and address the faithful.

For those Negroes who would subscribe to the Black Muslims except for their anti-Christian attitude, Muhammad has strong answers. He calls the Bible "the graveyard of my poor people." He quotes from the "poisoned book": "Love your enemies, bless them who curse you; pray for those who spitefully use you; him that smiteth thee on one cheek, offer him the other cheek . . . etc.," and then charges that "the Slavemasters couldn't have found a better teaching for their protection."

Muhammad says the Bible is suspect because it is dedicated to King James (a white man) rather than to God. He points out that the Bible "makes God guilty of an act of adultery by charging him with being the father of Mary's baby; it charges Noah with drunkenness and Lot with begetting children by his daughter. What a poison book. Christianity is a religion organized and backed by the white devils for the purpose of making slaves of black mankind. It has caused more bloodshed than any other combination of religions."

The Black Muslims welcomed the illiterate because they could than teach them according to the dictates of Muhammad. Muslim morality covers every detail of day-to-day living. The Muslim must pray five times a day: sunrise, noon, mid-afternoon, sundown, and before going to sleep—and even a sixth time if he wakes during the night. All prayers are made toward the east in the direction of the Holy City of Mecca. (Considering the distances from America, facing West could do as well.) Before each prayer, he must make the proper ablutions, rinsing his mouth, washing his hands, feet and forearms. Foods such as corn bread and pork are proscribed, as are many other foods common to the diet of poor Southern Negroes. Foods must be fresh "and decent," and in "no way resemble a slave diet."

The Muslim must attend at least two temple meetings a week, and, unless he has a good excuse for staying away and obtains permission, he may be summarily suspended. The men must also be prepared to "fish for the dead," a rather picturesque manner of saying that they must go out into the streets in search of new members. The Black Muslim is taught to elevate others of his race by elevating himself. Mutual responsibility and self-reliance are favorite exhortations of Muhammad. "Put your brains to work," he urges. "Think for self; walk in the direction of self; work for self and your children. Stop begging for what others have and help yourself to some of this good earth. We must go for ourselves." But with this, Muhammad commands his people to obey all constituted authority— "even the corrupt authority of the white man until the Black Nation returns to power." Women are especially warned not to imitate "the silly and often immoral habits of the white woman." They are regarded as equal in every way to their husbands but they are commanded to obey them, with modesty, thrift and service as their chief objectives in life.

In *Muhammad Speaks*, the official newspaper of the organization with a claimed circulation of "175,000 and still growing," a large amount of space is devoted to the women of Islam. They are advised to purchase Negro dolls for their little girls; to avoid wearing "pants or slacks" (a masculine man likes a feminine woman); to rely upon soap and water for their natural beauty instead of cosmetics; to keep their kitchens clean and their diet wholesome. A Negro menu and a Muslim diet are printed side by side. The Muslim diet favors lamb over ham; turnip greens over candied sweet potatoes; brown bread over white bread, and assorted fresh fruit over ordinary rich desserts.

In matters of sex, the publication prints articles repeatedly warning that mixed relations between blacks and whites cause disease and death. Morality is defined by ultra-puritanical standards. Infidelity or philandering is answerable to the strong-arm squad of the Fruit of Islam, which has quasi-judicial powers in this area. Courtship and marriage outside the Muslims are frowned upon, and, when a member does marry a non-member, unrelenting pressure is used upon the non-Muslim partner to join. Divorce is permitted, but strongly discouraged. A Muslim woman may not be alone in a room with a man except her husband. Muslim men are admonished to be especially alert for any manifestation of interest by a white man toward a Muslim woman. Venereal diseases and sex perversions are blamed solely on the white man's influence, and members are constantly warned that they face these two horrors if they persist in consorting with whites.

The Black Muslim philosophy stresses the regeneration of criminals and others who have fallen out with society. The organization has truly shown marked success in this field. Malcolm X declares that "when a man becomes a follower, no matter how bad his morals or habits were, he immediately takes upon himself a pronounced change which everyone admits. Muhammad has the magic of stopping them from being dope addicts, drunkards and thieves. I should like to think that this government would thank Mr. Muhammad for doing what it has failed to do toward rehabilitating men who have been classed as hardened criminals." Malcolm X cited instances in prisons where men, even after solitary confinements and other special punishment, did not improve until they became Muslims. "As soon as he becomes a Muslim," Malcolm X said, "he becomes a model prisoner, far more so than the so-called Negroes who confess Christianity." (It is to be noted that all Negroes except Muslims are referred to as "so-called Negroes.")

The uplifting of the Negro shows itself in its greatest appeal in the appearance and demeanor of its young and masculine leaders. The ministers are personable, dignified and sure of themselves without being smug or overbearing. All Muslims are clean-shaven, well-groomed in conservative clothes, and reserved. Inside the temples the ministers or the Fruit of Islam wear no uniforms or insignia except for a small star and crescent button in their lapels. Their attitude toward the "so-called Negroes" is one of toleration rather than condescension. They exude an atmosphere of muted force at the ready for the days when the Black Muslims will number 5,000,000, growing progressively larger and stronger.

This projected strength is openly expected to be translated into political action. Raymond Sharrieff, Supreme Captain of the Fruit of Islam, told a Detroit audience that "Muhammad plans to unite every stratum of the American Black Man—even if not a member of our temple. Religious, economic and political differences are luxuries that we

American Black Men cannot afford. We must sit together and counsel."

Political leaders of both parties are aware of the unified potential of the Black Muslims. An issue supported by Muhammad in a city with a large Negro population would find great strength with a Muslim bloc behind it. It is already accepted in New York's Harlem that Malcolm X is in a position to decide who will succeed Representative Adam Clayton Powell when he retires. Many political leaders of both colors have shown renewed interest and respect for the actions and pronouncements of Malcolm X. When Fidel Castro visited Harlem in 1960 he held a secret conference with Malcolm X that lasted two hours and ended with an invitation to the Muslim leader to visit Cuba. Muhammad rejected this because of his distaste for Communism. In other large cities such as Detroit, Philadelphia and Chicago, white political leaders and their Negro allies are carefully observing the growing power of the Muslims.

Unlike all other extremist groups, the Muslims do not wish to take over the United States. By their own words they want separation, not integration. But, until they achieve that, they will fight the black man's battle and extend their influence far beyond their official membership.

14. Rag, tag and bobtail

When the newspapers in the United States began giving prominent display to the seeming absurdities of Robert Welch and the John Birch Society and when important public figures commented on the resurgence of the Far Right, it was inevitable that this would bring out a number of persons who had been waiting for such an opportunity. These people are not axe-grinders. They are sincere citizens with secret grievances and the Far Right gives them the chance to voice these suppressed indignations.

One such platform is the new and rapidly growing National Indignation Convention, which was begun on an impulse by ex-fighter pilot Frank McGee in Dallas. He had seen a story that the United States was training Yugoslav aviators at Perrin Air Force Base in Texas, and he became so wroth that he spent $350 to hire a hall so he could voice his indignation. Almost a thousand citizens gathered in the Dallas Memorial Auditorium to hear him shout: "The United States is training Red Yugoslav pilots right here in

Texas. Now let's figure out what to do about this. As for me, I wouldn't give my enemy a bow and arrow."

Some people in the audience asked where the money came from to hire the auditorium. "The next thing I knew," McGee said, "a guy came to the edge of the balcony and started throwing down dollar bills. Then people were throwing coins and folding money, and guys were writing checks and floating them down on to the stage. I sent the stagehands out with pushbrooms to sweep them up. Not counting some that got sucked in by the air conditioning and some that maybe stuck to the brooms, we had $1,509."

It was an encouraging start, and McGee, a business man and former law student, is pushing hard at countless rallies to give people a chance to be indignant. The first objective of the N.I.C. is to force Congress to stop all military aid to any Communist country anywhere and to fire any government official responsible for any aid in the past. In the meantime the indignation is encouraged.

Mrs. Raymond Terwilliger, a red-haired housewife who is N.I.C. area coordinator, told a meeting in Freeport, New York: "I have just been told that Russian peat moss is being sold in many nurseries on Long Island. Remember to ask where your peat moss comes from."

Ronald Reagan, the film star, in a recorded message, denounced the "progressive income tax that was spawned by Karl Marx a hundred years ago."

Captain Eddie Rickenbacker used an N.I.C. rally to praise the late Senator McCarthy, who "had the courage to oppose the enemy and realized that the method had to be drastic to bring attention . . . Some day the American people will erect a monument to his memory."

Fluoridation, public welfare and other social legislation are denounced with verve and enthusiasm, and McGee feels that things must be improved if enough people become indignant.

The Reverend Gerald L. K. Smith's Christian Nationalist Crusade states its credo thus:

10 HIGH PRINCIPLES

The ten high principles on which the Christian Nationalist Crusade rests are as follows:

1. Preserve America as a Christian Nation, being conscious of the fact that there is a highly organized campaign to substitute Jewish tradition for Christian tradition.
2. Expose, fight and outlaw Communism.
3. Safeguard American liberty against the menace of bureaucratic Fascism.
4. Maintain a government set up by the majority which abuses no minority and is abused by no minority. Fight mongrelization and all attempts being made to force the intermixture of the black and white races.
5. Protect and earmark national resources for our citizenry first.
6. Maintain the George Washington Foreign Policy of friendship with all nations, trade with all nations, entangling alliances with none.
7. Oppose a world government and a super-state.
8. Prove that the Worker, the Farmer, the Businessman, the Veteran, the Unemployed, the Aged, and the Infirm can enjoy more abundance under the American system than

any alien system now being proposed by foreign propagandists.

9. Safeguard America's tradition in relationship to immigration.

10. Enforce the Constitution as it pertains to our monetary system.

In special bulletins from the Crusade's under-cover Washington agents and in each month's issue of *The Cross and the Flag,* Smith recites harrowing instances of the multiple conspiracy to de-Christianize and mongrelize the country. The same rumors of Presidential disease used against Roosevelt are directed against Kennedy—flat statements that he is constantly under the influence of "strong medicines." The old women of both sexes who make up a large part of the magazine's subscription list are also told:

> Our beautiful Capital city has been seized by Negroes. The population is nearly three-fourths black. The school population is nearly 80% black.
>
> The Jews are in command of the Executive Department and the Supreme Court.
>
> The liquidation of General Edwin A. Walker is . . . part of a diabolical appeasement policy which characterizes the Fabian Socialists in power.
>
> Felix Frankfurter, the mentor of Alger Hiss and his fraternity of Marxist mind-washers, is the boss of the Supreme Court. Earl Warren, the Chief Justice, serves him like a spineless puppet.

One of Smith's more ingenious fantasies is the diabolical plot of the Chinese Communists and Fidel Castro to enslave the United States by making every American a dope addict. (A month later Smith admitted that the Chinese had not discovered narcotics: it was an international Jewish cabal, based in Europe and Britain, that had made addicts of the Chinese and that was planning to conquer Christendom with opium and heroin.) According to Smith's paper, press-gangs roam Communist China rounding up homeless men, who are chained in the holds of ships and relentlessly pumped full of heroin until they are confirmed addicts. These ships then enter American ports and disgorge the infected hordes. Each man is told that he cannot get another injection until he has brought a new addict back to his ship. Naturally, the poor coolies are so frenzied for a *fix* that even the barriers of immigration laws and language cannot stand against them.

But Smith also has one isolated platoon of pet Jews. This is the American Jewish League Against Communism, and Smith's special pet is its Los Angeles leader, Rabbi Max Merritt. An indication of the League's influence beyond the angelic city may be derived from the fact that no well informed Jews could identify the good man of God or recall any pertinent information about his League.

The Conservative Society of America is operated by Kent Courtney, a former airline pilot, who weighs 240 pounds, and his Junoesque wife, Phoebe. "The Birch Society is educational," Courtney explains, "and we are political. They tell them what's wrong and we tell them what to do."

With headquarters in New Orleans, the Courtneys run a newspaper, *The Independent American*, which sells for 25 cents, and publishes, among other items, a voting record of Congressmen to test their fidelity to the cause. So far only

38 out of 437 Senators and Representatives have qualified. The Society also publishes pamphlets with the frank titles of *Is Foreign Aid a Fantastic Fraud? The Income Tax Can Be Repealed; Is Goldwater Really a Conservative?* The Courtneys no longer believe Goldwater qualifies for the Right and have directed their enthusiasm toward ex-Major General Walker.

"He is the one," Phoebe Courtney says. "Just wait till he tastes blood and the little old ladies start pawing him." But they were doomed to disappointment in Walker, who could never understand that civilians cannot be ordered to jump, as paratroopers are, and depended on to jump without question. The Courtneys are certain that somewhere in the land there is another man who will combine the glamor of Walker and the cunning of Goldwater and who will be nothing but a Rightist. Meanwhile, the money keeps coming in and the Courtneys continue to tell their followers how to pressure their Congressmen toward the Right. Subscriptions to their publications, plus small donations, add up to more than $200,000 a year.

J. Evetts Haley looks like a moving-picture version of a Big Texan. He has that tall, lean and wiry look, sports a ten-gallon hat of pure white and repeats at every opportunity that he wants to hang Chief Justice Warren. A man of this type could be swiftly dismissed as the distillation of all crackpots, but as head of Texans for America he has wrought the kind of vicious mischief that even the John Birch Society has not been able to achieve. The specialty of his organization is to snoop out Communist subversion in Texas school books. He scored a most disturbing success in 1961 when every history textbook adopted by the Texas

Education Agency was altered to meet his organization's demands.

"I'm a newcomer to the ranks of the book-burners," he likes to boast. "This academic freedom stuff is all wrong. The stressing of both sides of a controversy only confuses the young and encourages them to make snap judgments. Until they are old enough to understand they should be taught only the American side."

Haley has another fear, which is developing into a hysteria. He feels that the food and medicine the United States is sending to underdeveloped countries is helping extend the life of backward people "who could some day outnumber us and destroy us." There should be some control, he insists, that will limit the development of those countries "so they can be kept in their place and never become a threat to us." To him, India and the new African countries are the ones we must observe as potential enemies.

The Far Right has offered a gratifying outlet to some military men, who by nature and training are men of action and cannot quietly face the frustrating inaction of a Cold War with the attendant political restrictions. While ex-Major General Walker took his stand when he was still on active duty, the others waited until they had retired. Then they joined the American Security Council, which makes carefully detailed studies on vital national security issues and offers recommendations. Among the military men who are members are General Albert C. Wedemeyer, Lieutenant General Edward M. Almond, Admiral Felix B. Stump, Admiral Ben Moreell, Admiral Arthur B. Radford, the former chairman of the Joint Chiefs of Staff, and Rear Admiral Chester Ward—all retired.

General Wedemeyer explained the resurgence of the Rightist movement by saying that "heat generates heat— extremism begets extremism." He feels that there should be no stopping of free discussion by the military on military matters, but "I believe that military men on active duty should not get involved in politics."

Brigadier General Bonner Fellers, retired, a wartime aide to General Douglas MacArthur, is a national director of an organization called For America, and chairman of the Citizens' Foreign Aid Committee, which opposes foreign aid on the ground that "when a President of the United States extends foreign aid to an underdeveloped country he is motivated by a desire for personal influence —and there should be no personal element in this kind of policy."

Where some military men fall into the category of irresponsibles is in their views on the use of nuclear weapons. Many, like Walker, feel that the civilians who run the United States are not equipped by training to understand the value of certain weapons. Fellers has said that nuclear arms should be used in South Vietnam and Laos. While he stops at this point, there are others who feel that a preventive nuclear war now would be best for America. Others feel that the United States should have made this move years ago. These men speak with dignity and conviction and they have the stature and background to persuade their listeners that theirs is the only way—ignoring the legal and traditional American concept that the commander-in-chief of all the military should be an elected civilian.

Opposition to censorship of the military under any con-

ditions is a fixed stand of the Daughters of the American
Revolution, whose Rightist hierarchy goes babbling on its
zany way without the least regard to the passage of time
or the needs of the nation. They can be counted upon at
every annual convention to adopt resolutions that would
stop the clock of progress and keep America pure from foreign entanglements. Medical care for the aged under Social Security is the most recent "horror" to which the
D.A.R. is opposed. The ladies see the black hand of Fabian
Socialism in every piece of progressive legislation, mistrust
the United Nations and fear any attempt at disarmament.
They support the restrictive Immigration and Nationality
Act as a first line of defense against all foreigners and are
definitely against any reduction in the tariff.

The D.A.R. believes in democracy as long as that does
not interfere with its own functions. As a result, there is
rebellion in the ranks for the first time in many years. All
the resolutions are formulated by the D.A.R.'s 51-member
resolutions committee and are generally adopted without
protest from the floor of the Continental Congress, the
name given to the annual convention. Should any member
wish to introduce or amend a resolution from the floor, she
is ruled out of order. Quite a number of women have resigned from time to time because they could not subscribe
to the content or the tenor of the resolutions. One of the
most significant resignations was that of Mrs. Ernest Ives,
sister of Adlai Stevenson, who felt that she was ineffectual
against the solidly Right hierarchy.

But one who did not resign was Mrs. Dennis E. Kent,
regent of the Chappaqua Chapter in New York's West-
chester County, who maintained that "you can't fight them

from the outside. I think our organization needs saving, and it must be done in the present tense." After being ruled out of order when she suggested that all resolutions be first considered by local chapters, Mrs. Kent pledged to continue her battle in the future. "All my members are with me in this," she said. "Our quarrel is not so much with the resolutions as with the method by which they are handled." It was encouraging to note that Mrs. Kent received some support from other members, and, while her strength is not yet known, there is the hope that the D.A.R. may be facing a revolution of its own in years to come.

One of the oldest established right-wing views is expressed by Dr. Clarence E. Manion, a former dean of the Note Dame University Law School, who started out as a New Dealer, became an aide to President Eisenhower, and ended as head of the Manion Forum, which costs $10,000 a week to operate and spouts standard Rightist propaganda.

Manion, a Kentuckian, vintage 1896, served in the First World War, joined the Notre Dame faculty in 1924 and resigned as dean in 1952 "because of pressure of private business." He left the Democrats to support Senator Taft for the Republican nomination for the Presidency. Eisenhower appointed him chairman of the Commission on Inter-Governmental Relations at the request of Sherman Adams, who made the recommendation in order to keep peace in the Republican family. It did not work out as Adams had hoped. Manion spent too much time away from his duties on lecture tours in which he attacked the Tennessee Valley Authority and urged support for the proposed amendment to the Constitution, which would have limited the treaty-making powers of the President. Despite the formal language, President Eisenhower fired Manion, arousing to wrath a number of regulars in the right-wing movement, including some hard-core American Firsters.

Under the indignant leadership of the late Colonel Robert R. McCormick, the ultra-nationalist then publisher of the Chicago *Tribune*, and Hamilton Fish, a former New York Representative, an organization called For America was formed with Manion as co-chairman. The other chairman was Robert W. Wood, retired chairman of Sears Roebuck and Co., and a former chairman of the America First Committee. The new group won the immediate praise of Senator McCarthy, who said "it would be very healthy sometime to get a realignment of parties so there would be no extreme left wing or right wing in either the Republican or Democratic Parties."

As a possible third party, the organization faded rapidly from view, but Manion in his forum continues adamantly to espouse and publicize every rightist platitude that was ever uttered. When the Birch Society was founded he became a member of its executive committee because its line was perfectly suited to him.

There are countless other extremist groups on the Right and Left, such as the remnants of the old Trotskyite splinter and the various little hate groups. They operate furtively, spying on their neighbors, playing a dangerous little game called *Patriots and Communists* and causing a great deal of minor mischief.

Robert G. Spivack, columnist in the New York *Herald Tribune*, after a study of these rightist anomalies, observed: "When the public is frustrated in its desires for tranquility, comfort and easier times, when everything seems to be falling apart . . . the tendency is to look for a national scapegoat. Many of these political activists are fanatics, and fanaticism can produce cruel results. Several incidents . . . prove this. The attack on a young applicant to the Peace Corps who was obstreperous at a Rotary Club meeting was built up far out of proportion to its seriousness. Fanaticism does strange things to people—especially when it destroys the very things they love."

15. What makes them rant

Extremism is not new in the United States. Side by side with our democratic traditions has run a persistent mistrust of democracy. It first showed itself when the American Party, better remembered as the Know-Nothing Party, fed on the anti-foreigner sentiment, and for a while managed to control several state governments and Congressmen. In 1856, its Presidential candidate, Millard Fillmore, captured one-fifth of the popular vote, but after that the Know-Nothings faded from the scene.

There were many, like the Ku Klux Klan, the Silver Shirts, Fritz Kuhn's German-American Bund, Father Coughlin's Christian Front, and others that feasted on racism, anti-Semitism, anti-Catholicism and anti-anything that resembled social progress.

Franklin Roosevelt's liberal legislation brought about the birth of the Liberty League, which was dedicated to opposing anything that departed from the policy of President McKinley. The Liberty League is regarded as the direct ancestor of Taft and Goldwater conservatism. The America

Firsters functioned for a while, fighting for unrealistic isolationism, but left the scene when it was obvious that the United States was an integral part of this world and nothing would change that.

The rebirth of the extreme right wing came after World War II, when the United States and the Soviet Union began the classic stalemate known as the Cold War. People began to realize that these two countries held the key to world peace and that there was no simple solution to reconcile their monumental differences.

It is the absence of the simple solution that has accelerated the growth of the far and irresponsible right. The old familiar landmarks have been disappearing for thirty years. At home, the New Frontier has aroused almost as much hostility as the New Deal that preceded it. In the world, colonialism is vanishing. Again at home, there is for many a disturbing parallel in the emergence of a disturbing new force transforming race relations. Russia has flaunted demonstration after frightening demonstration of her power, crushing the first revolt of a terrestrial satellite and putting the first unmanned and manned space satellites into orbit. America is no longer the accepted champion in every undertaking, scientific, economic or political. And for more than 15 years the world has waited for nuclear war.

The average American has comported himself creditably, supporting or opposing his Government's policies and programs within the framework of his chosen party, eager to consider any suggestion that may ease the tensions and the threats. But, according to students of human behavior, there is a residue of less than three per cent of the population that reacts very differently.

The psychology of the demagogue has been exhaustively explored by experts. Often he is no more than an unscrupulous quester for power, fame or wealth; almost as often he is varyingly pathological if not psychopathic. In either case he may or may not be "sincere." This would be irrelevant except that too often "sincerity" may make him the more dangerous, for the true fanatic is far less likely than the opportunist to know when to stop. For some, dispassionate study, for others, inborn flair has ferreted out the fears and desires of the three per cent of the population to whom they must initially appeal. It is these dupes who are the nucleus of the mob that every demagogue hopes to incite and believes he can forever manipulate.

Basically, they are frustrated and frightened—frustrated within themselves regardless of their seeming external "success" and frightened that what they have may be taken from them or that what they seek may be snatched out of their reach. Many have suffered real losses, through the fault of themselves, of others or of circumstances; many have suffered even worse losses, the losses of fantasy—and both kinds of losers seek revenge and retribution. A deep inferiority claims them all; in some the lack of identity is so aching that only in clinging to a group of their compeers can they find a semblance of selfhood. This is as true of the rank-and-file of the far left as of that of the far right, and it applies equally to many of the intellectuals at both extremes, who have somehow lost the image of self in the pursuit of the abstract. In the great mass there is the fear, as old as the race, of anyone or anything that is "different" or "superior."

Paranoia and paranoid delusions, especially of some sinister *they* or *it*, are profoundly rooted in the political extremist's personality. He is chronically suspicious that *it* or *they* will seize "control"—of him and of all he cherishes. In paranoia, the attribution of "evil" to outside forces is a projection of the individual's own "evil"—unacceptable—desires and impulses, which his unconscious inner censor cannot tolerate in himself and which he must therefore attribute to others. In the very manner in which he denounces *them* and the protective measures he proposes or advocates, he betrays his own unconscious lust to control and rule and to practice against those whom he has designated enemies the very deprivation of life, property and liberty of which he accuses them.

Such fear, suspicion and repressive wishes manifest themselves in extremist denunciation of the United Nations (which must be destroyed before it destroys America), of various kinds of taxation (which again are branded "destructive"), of the Supreme Court (a menace to be resolved only by the elimination of incumbent personnel), of Negroes or Catholics or Jews (each of whom seeks to rule "us" and must therefore be thrust into subjection or exile); even fluoridation of drinking water and campaigns for mental hygiene become, in the eyes of the political paranoid, the insidious weapons by which the enemy of the American way of life seeks to destroy the nation's physical health and undermine its intellectual integrity. This belief that everything that frightens is an instrument of a vicious conspiracy is first cousin to the psychotic paranoiac's conviction that someone or something is attacking him with invisible powerful "rays" designed to subjugate him and the entire world.

Not all such paranoids and paranoiacs are merely the raggle-taggle of society. They are often men and women of outstanding, even brilliant intellectual and professional achievement. What unites the soldiers of this psychopathic army, from subway motorman to corporation executive and university professor, is the unshakable conviction that, somewhere where no one can penetrate or act, the dreadful *they* plot night and day to destroy all that is good and right.

But the fearful and the suspicious are not alone. They stand beside the outright megalomaniac psychopaths—often people of considerable intellectual endowment but essentially conscienceless and cruel. The archetype in the 1920's was perhaps Gerald Chapman, the millionaire's son who chose gangsterism as a career and died in the electric chair. These people are hateful and sadistic; at the same time they are inordinately infantile and narcissistic, intoxicated by the power to be derived from controlling others. Such men become Dillingers, Schultzes, Capones; on a more elevated and civilized scale they become—or aspire to be— Napoleons or Bismarcks or Alexanders. This is the personality of a Rockwell; when it is complicated by paranoia, it is the personality of a Hitler.

But perhaps the majority of the followers of extremist agitators, whether of the right or of the left, are those whom the psychiatrists call the "inadequate personalities." These are the people who have never been able to "make it," even in the lowest levels of meeting the problems of life: the drifters, the punks who must sporadically erupt in emotional or physical violence, the petty thieves and gyps, the perennially idle, the pathologically self-indulgent. All of them are consumed with a sickening conviction—and a valid one—of their own individual worthlessness; they have no reservoir of inner strength to enable them to take the responsibility for their situation and to try to cope with it. So they blame the "system," the Negroes, the Catholic Church, the Jews, the Communists, the "big guys." These are the raw material for the lynch mobs that the extremist agitators hope to organize, exploit, control and, when they have served their purpose, erase.

Index